DANCE CREATIONS
COLORING BOOK
VOLUME I
THIRTY DRAWINGS
TO COLOR

I0475235

FIRST EDITION

THANK YOU VERY MUCH FOR PURCHASING THIS COLORING BOOK.

DESIGNED FOR BOTH THE BEGINNER AND INTERMEDIATE

COLORING LEVELS, THIS COLORING BOOK FEATURES

SOME OF MY BEST DANCE-THEMED DRAWINGS.

ENJOY, AND LET YOUR ARTISTIC SIDE SHINE THROUGH!

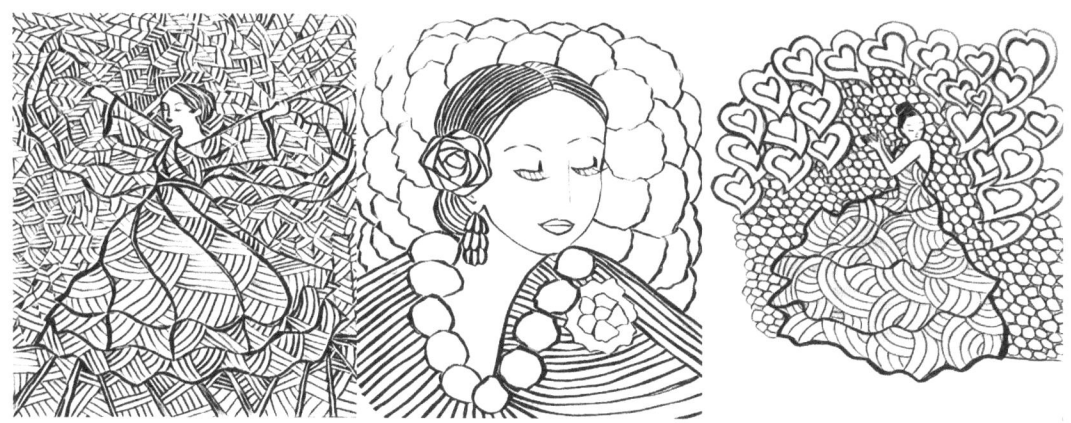

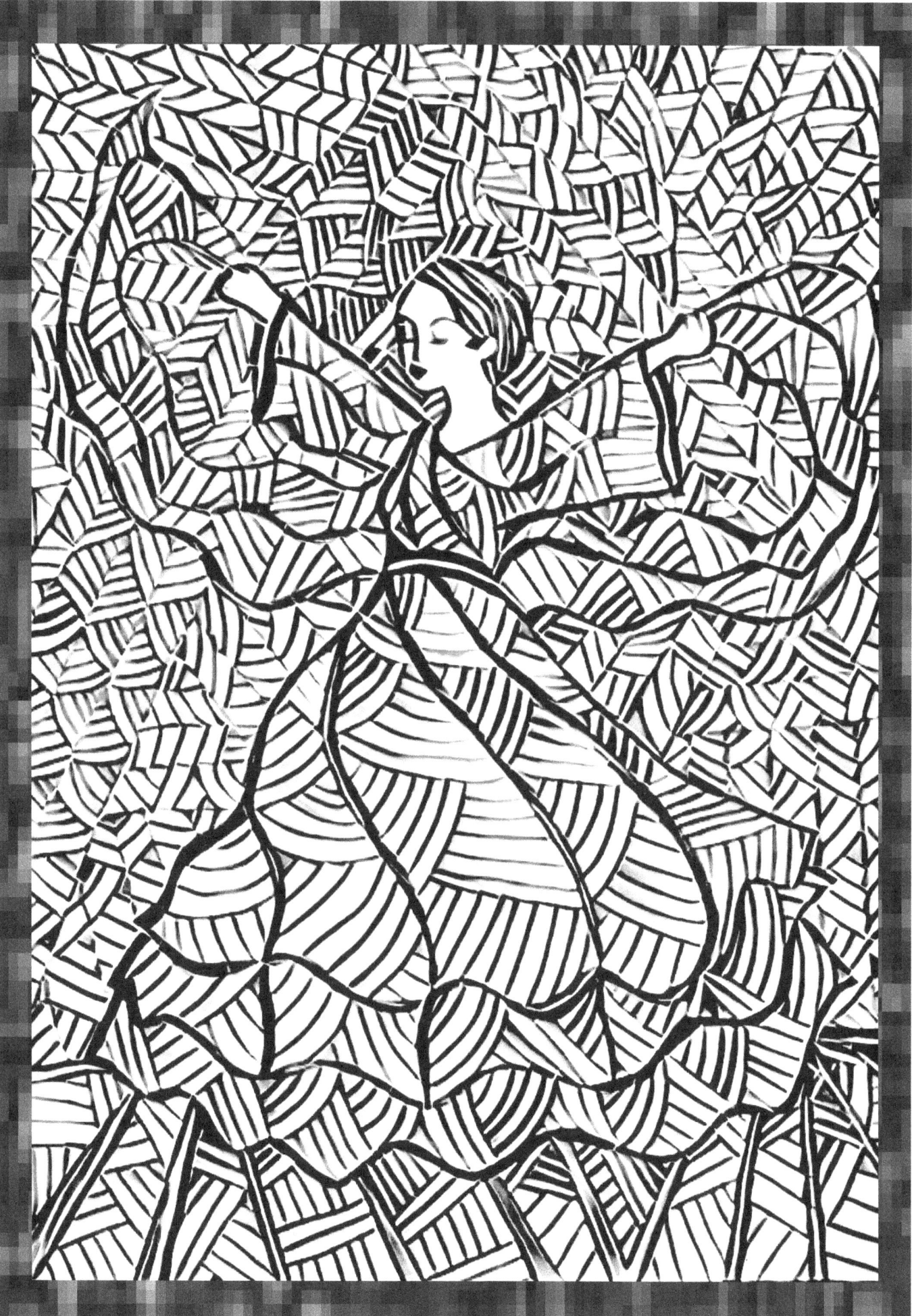

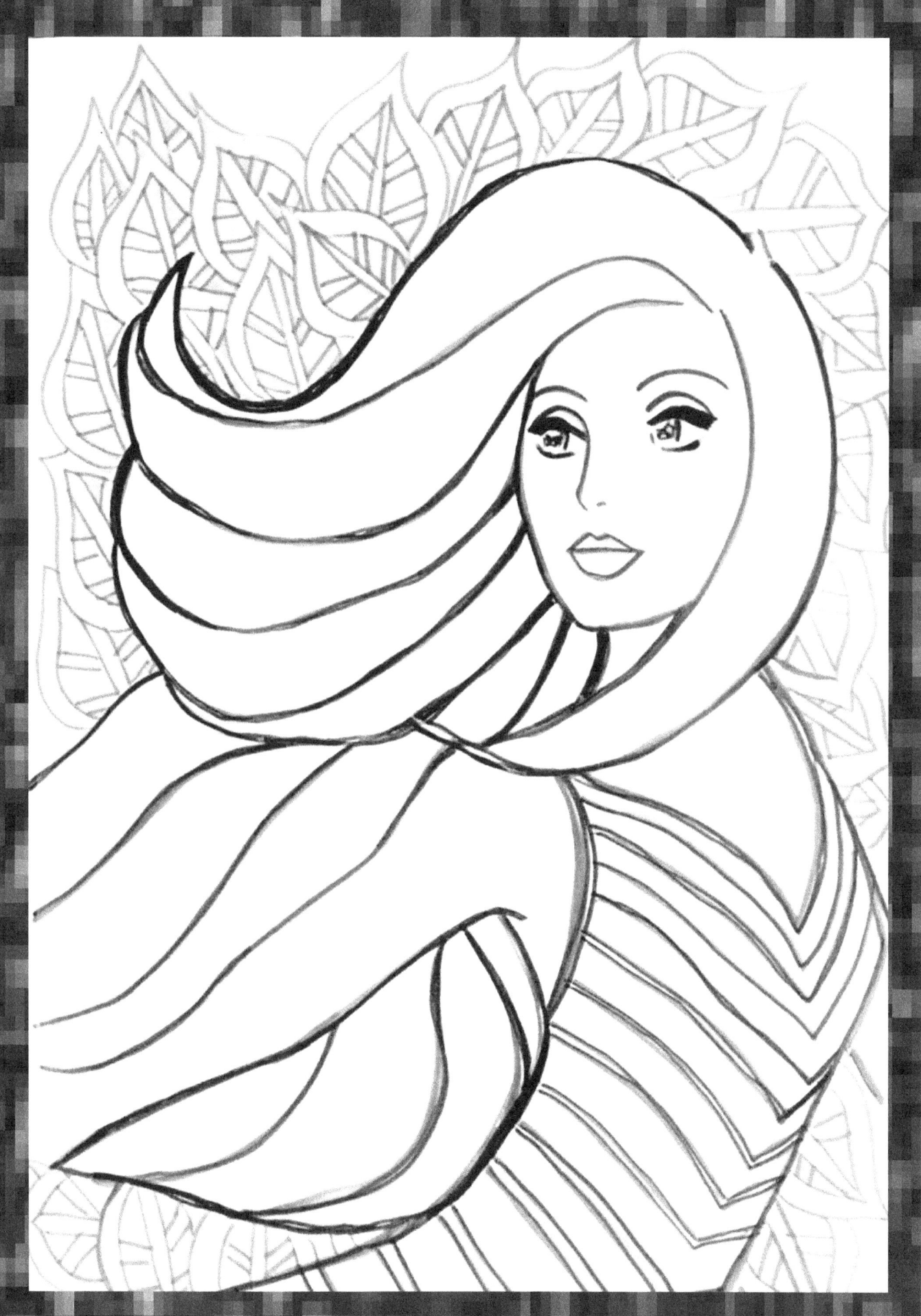

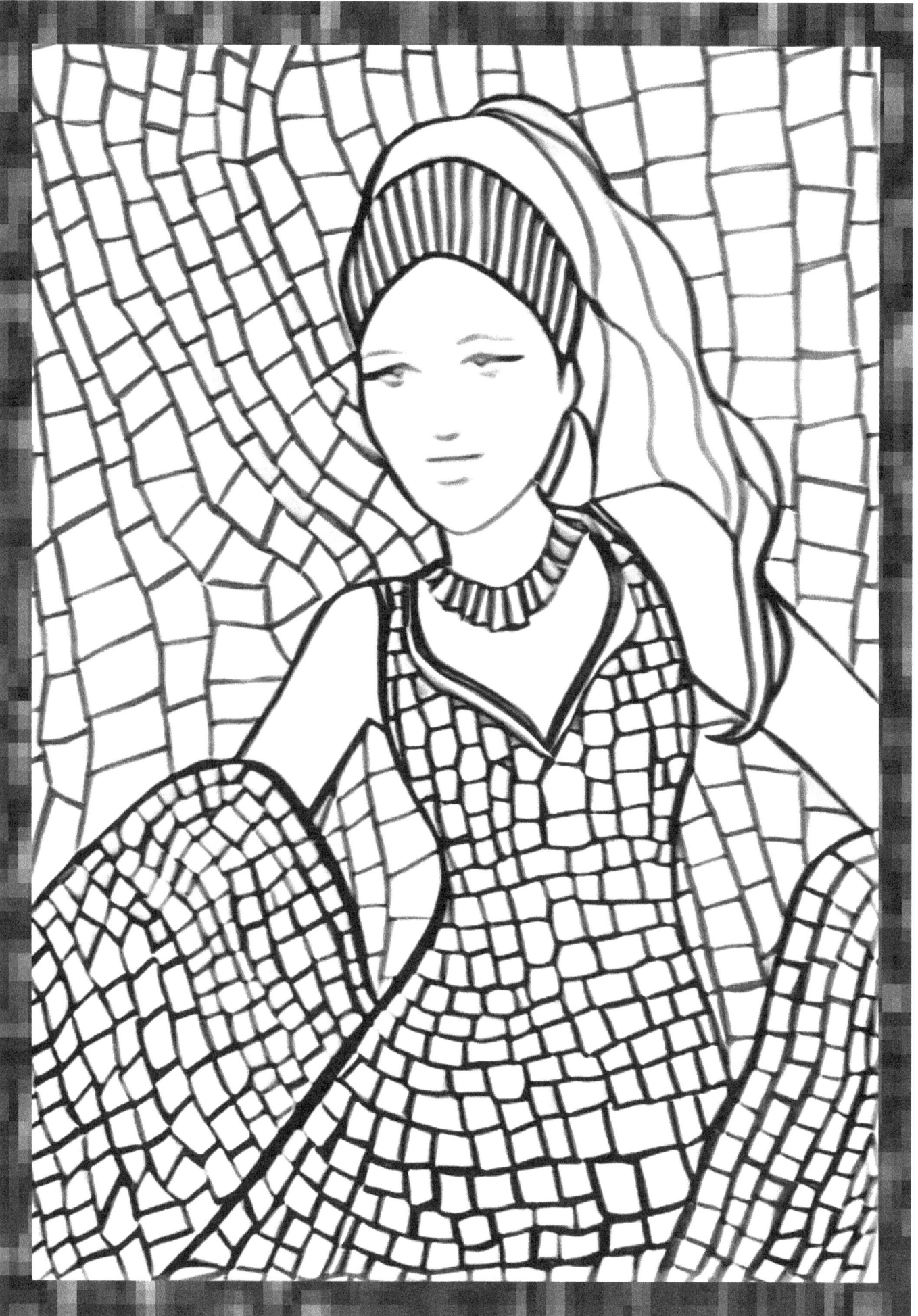

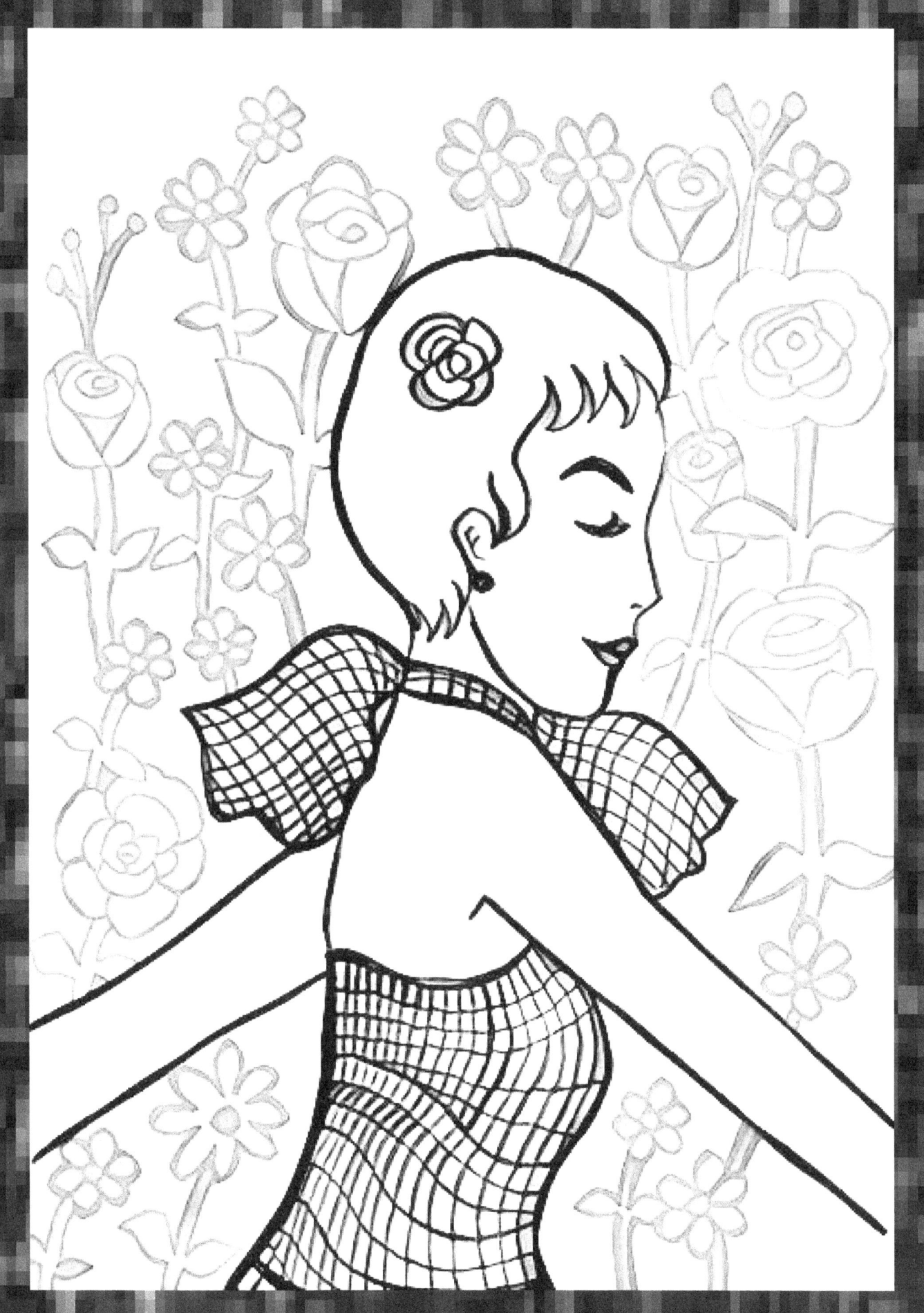

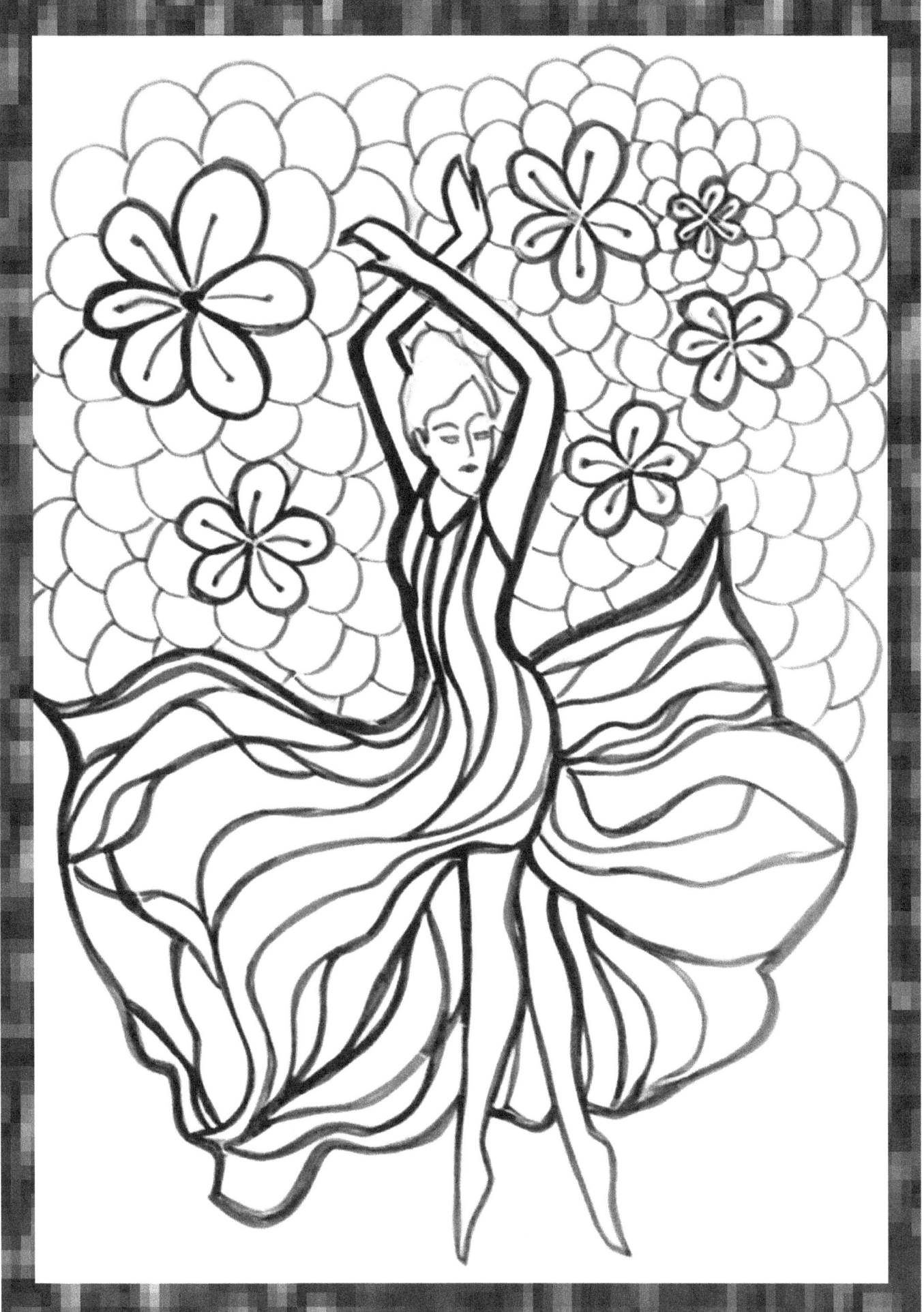

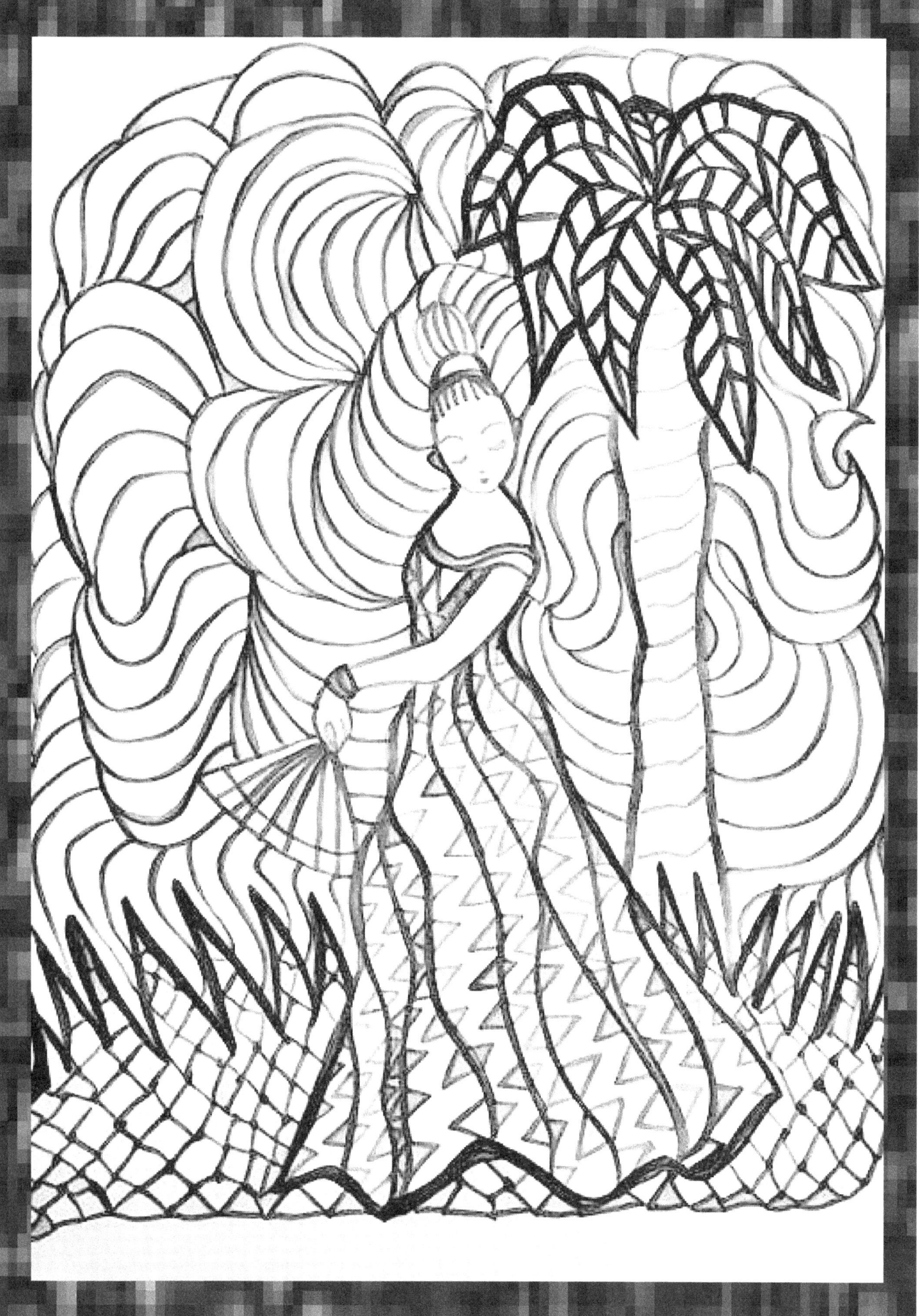

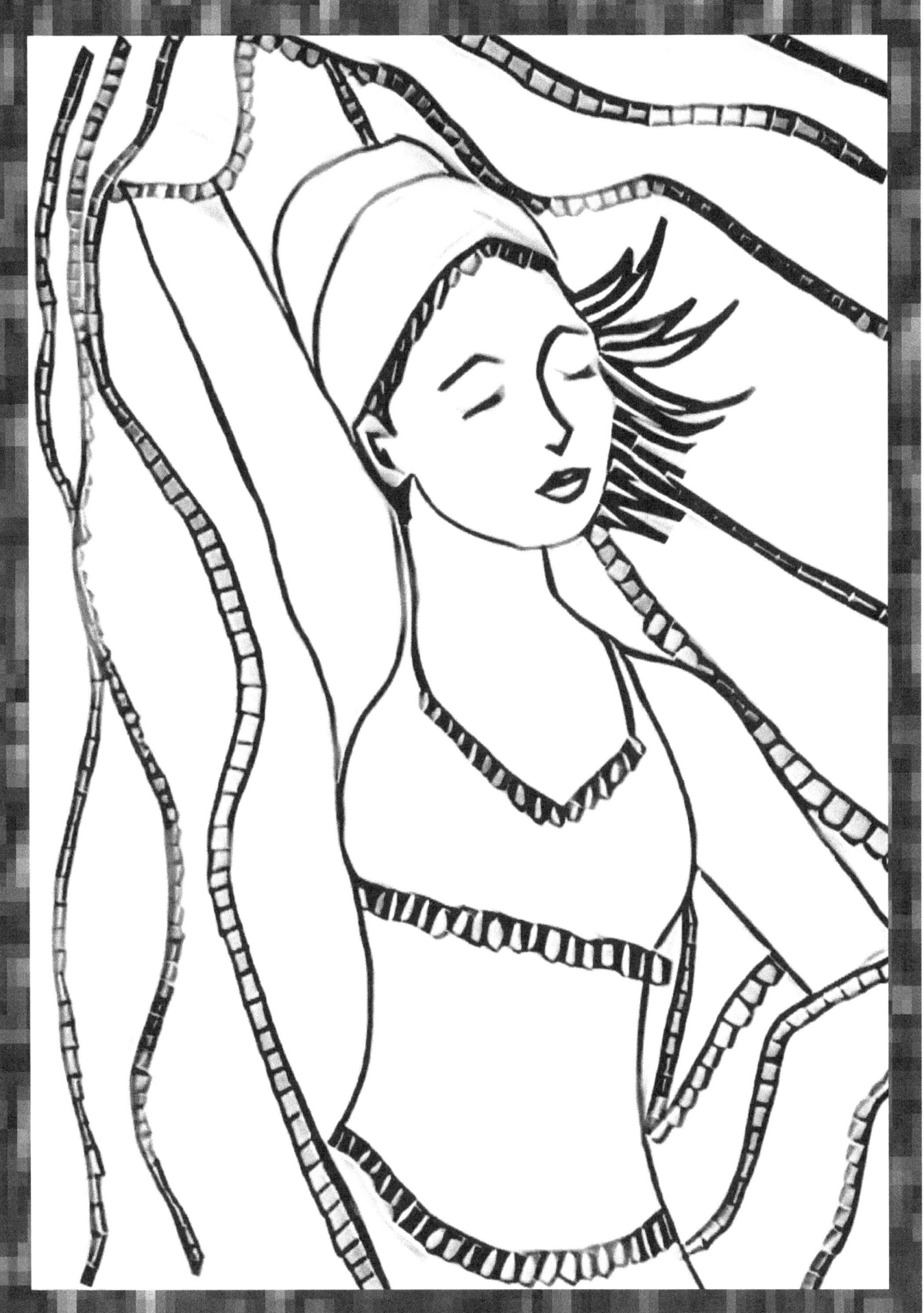

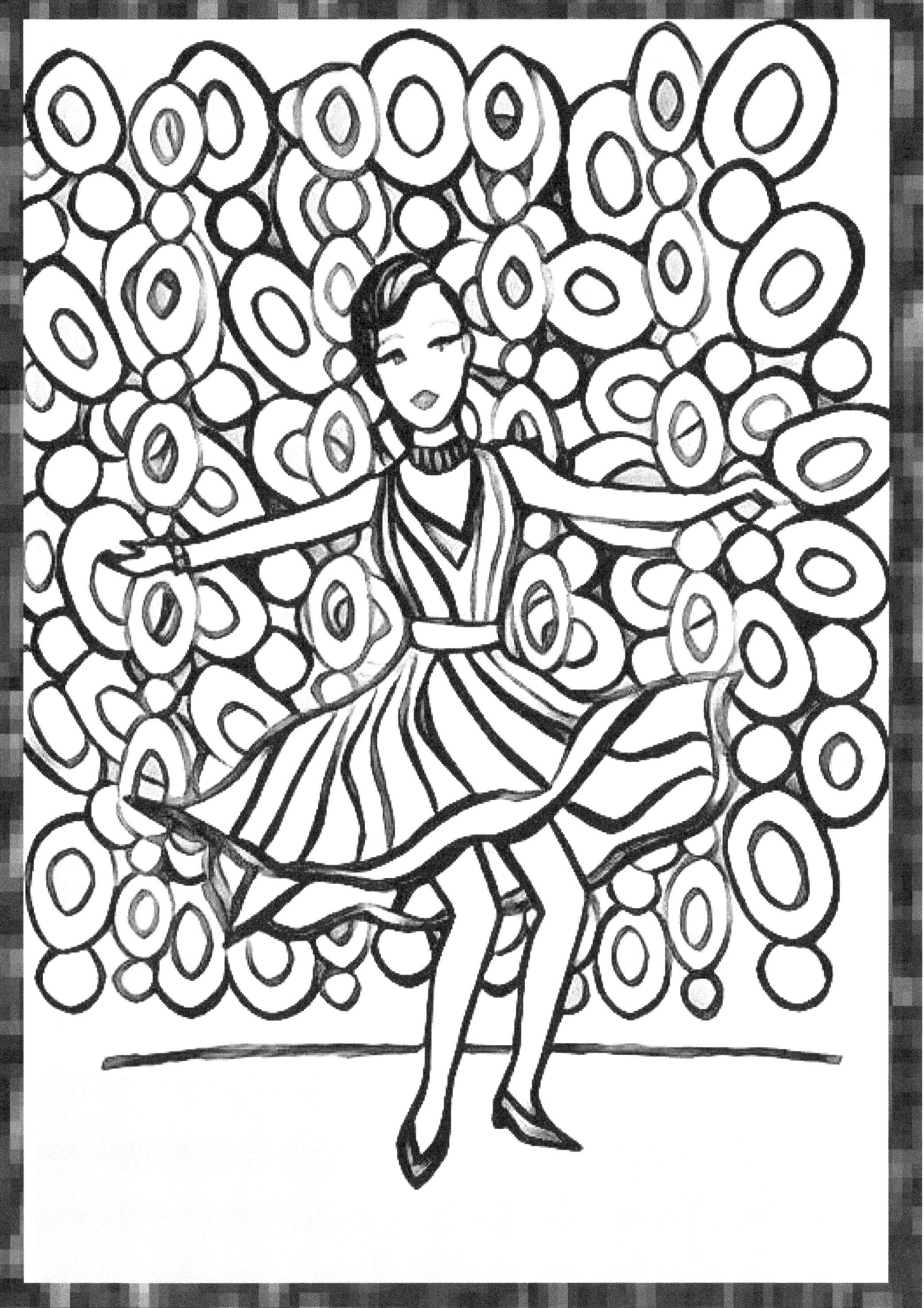

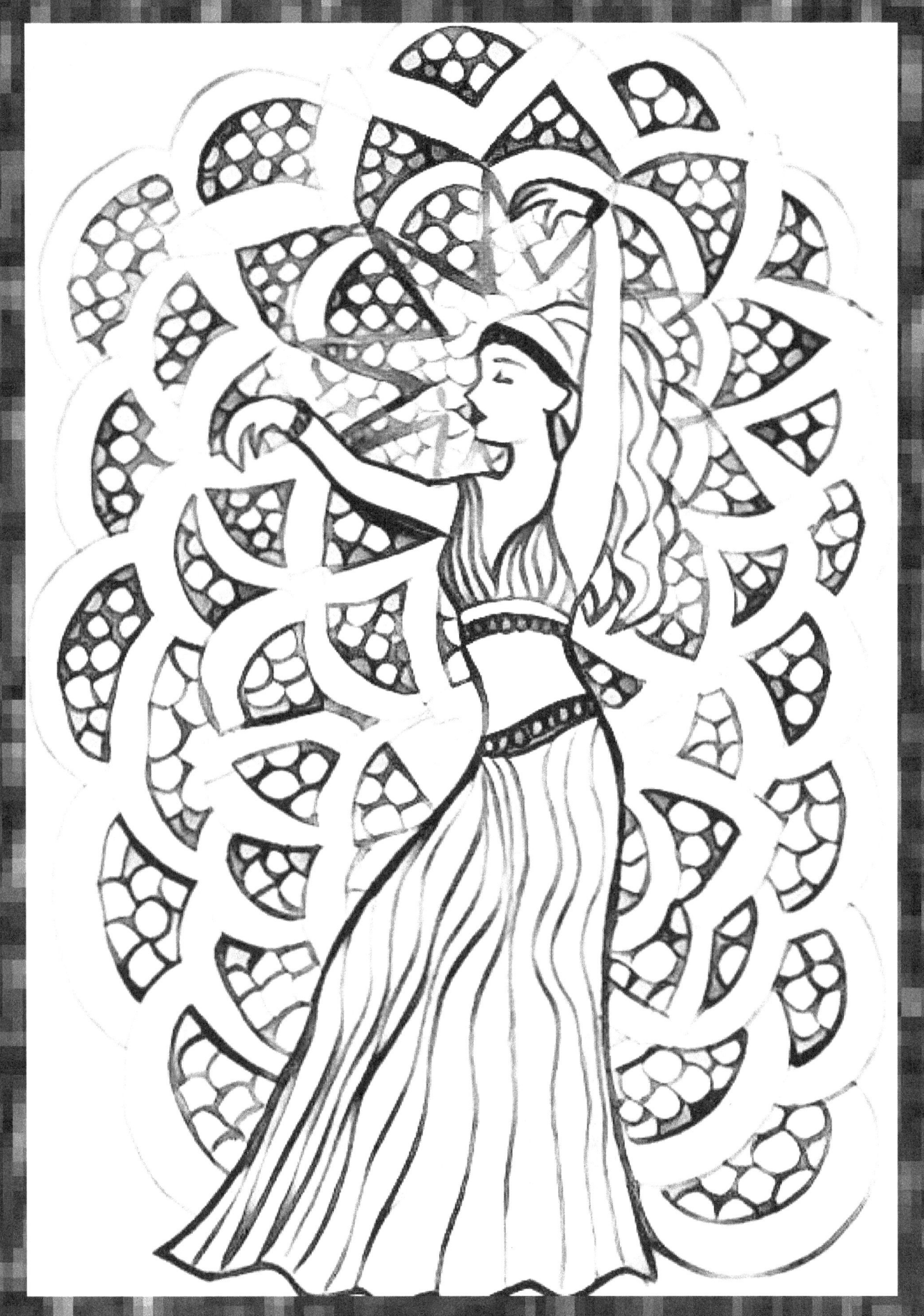

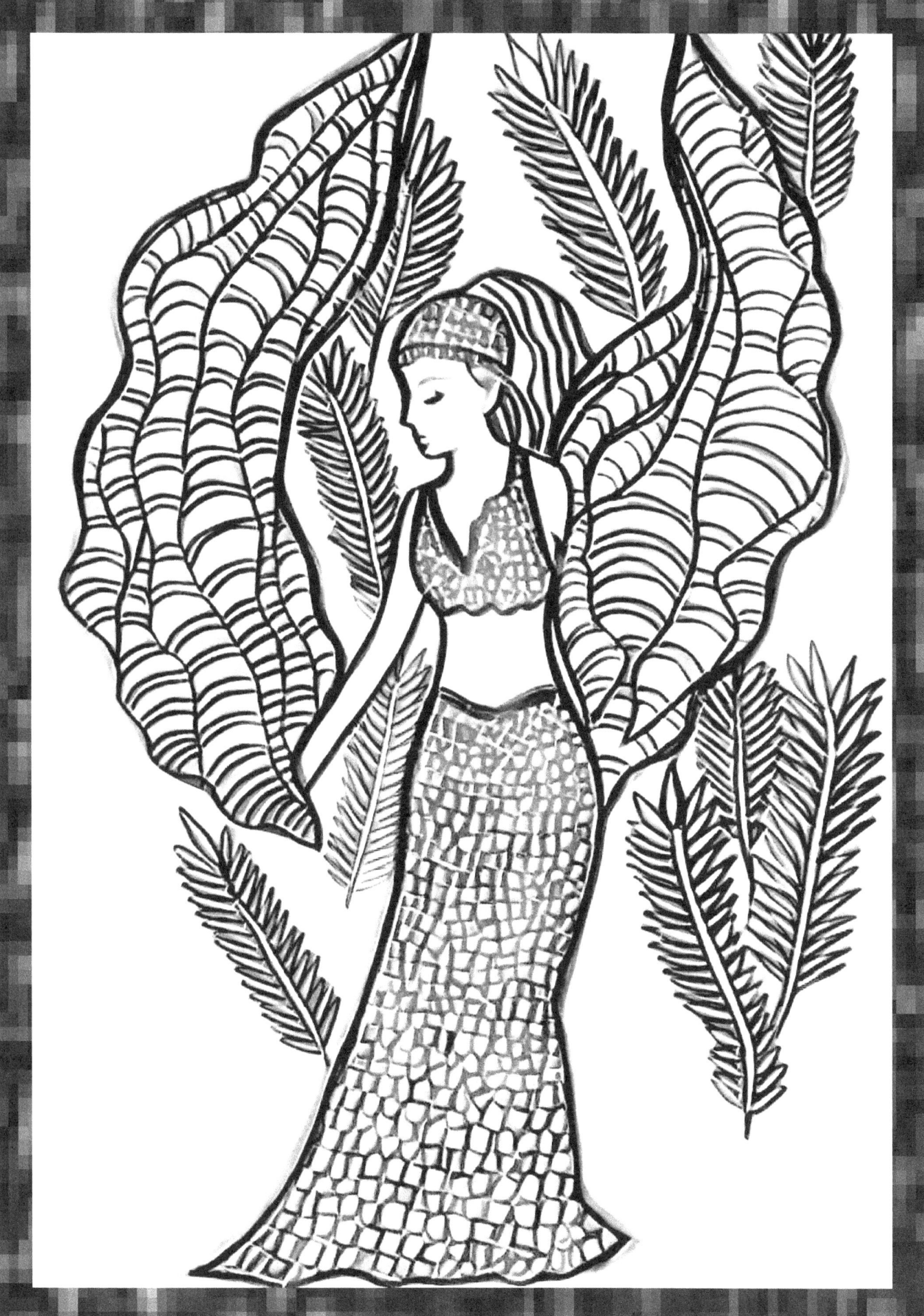

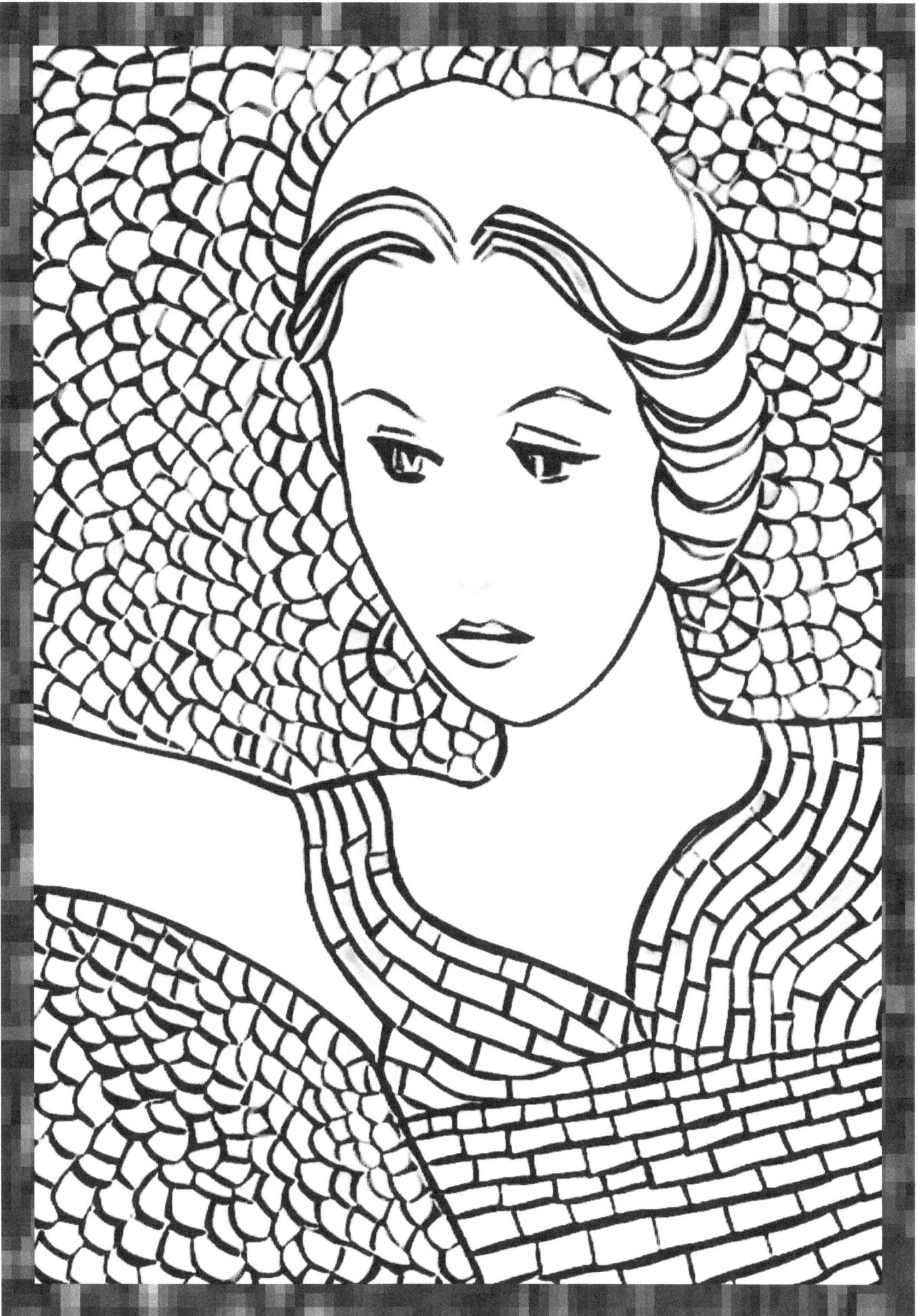

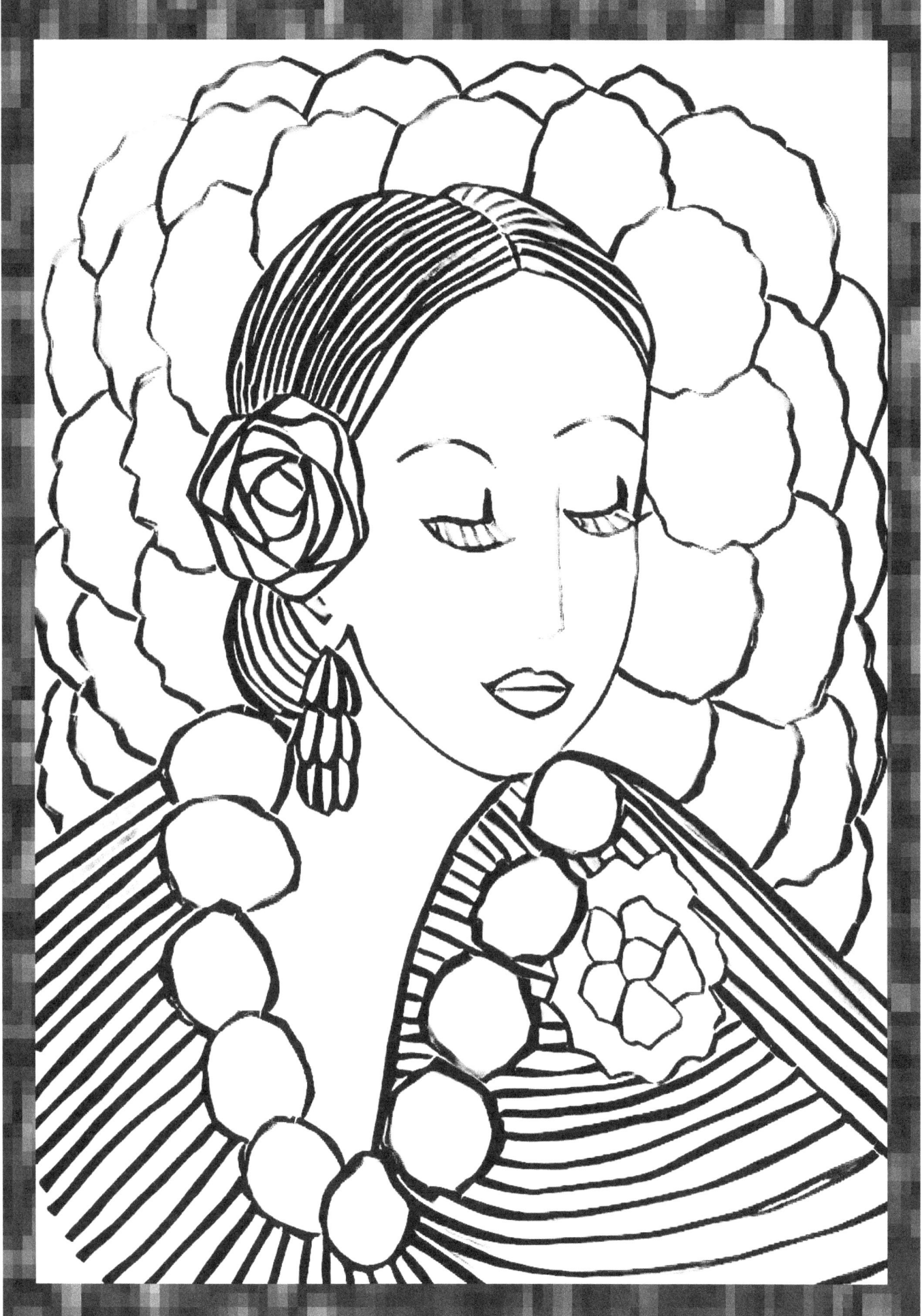

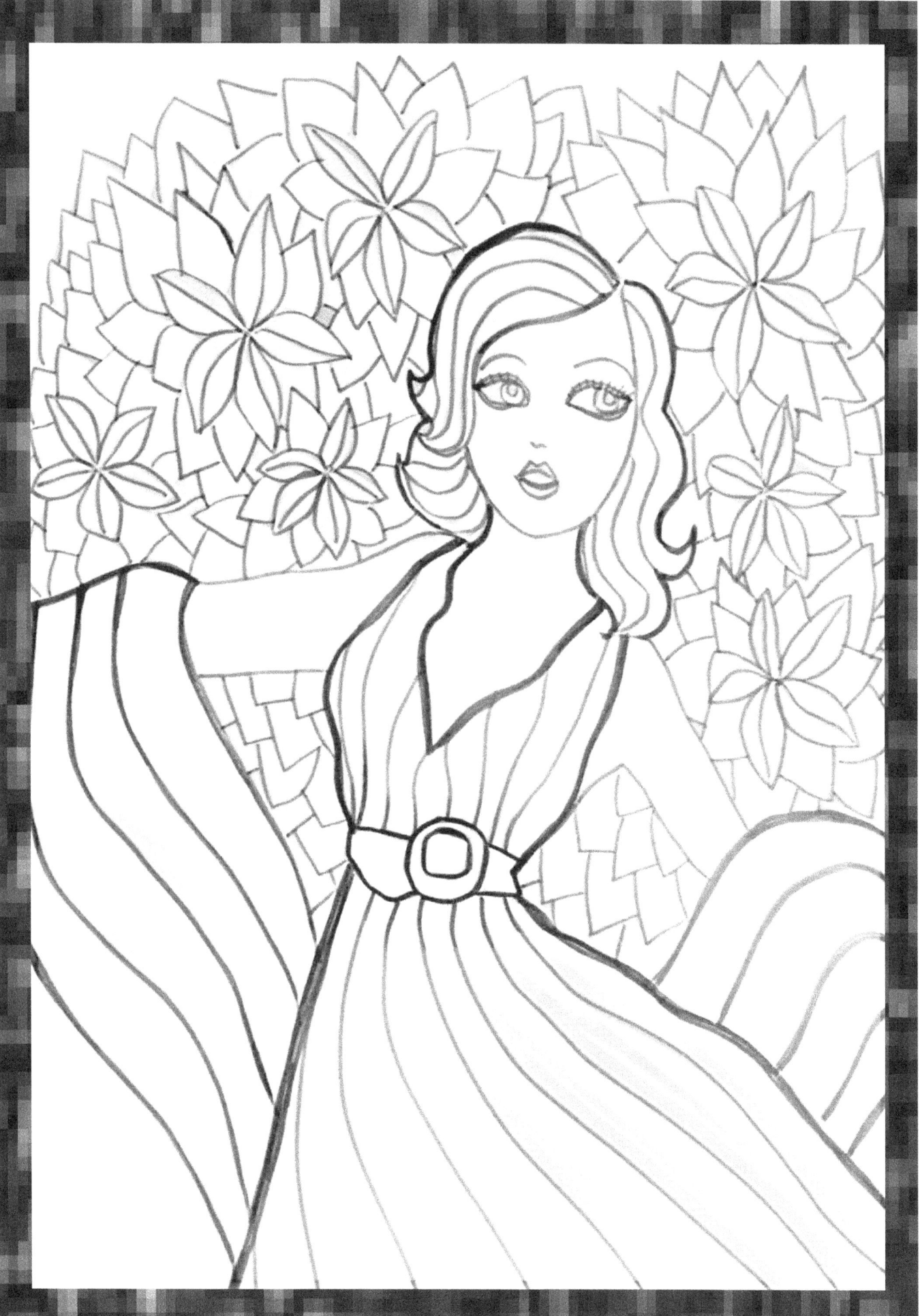

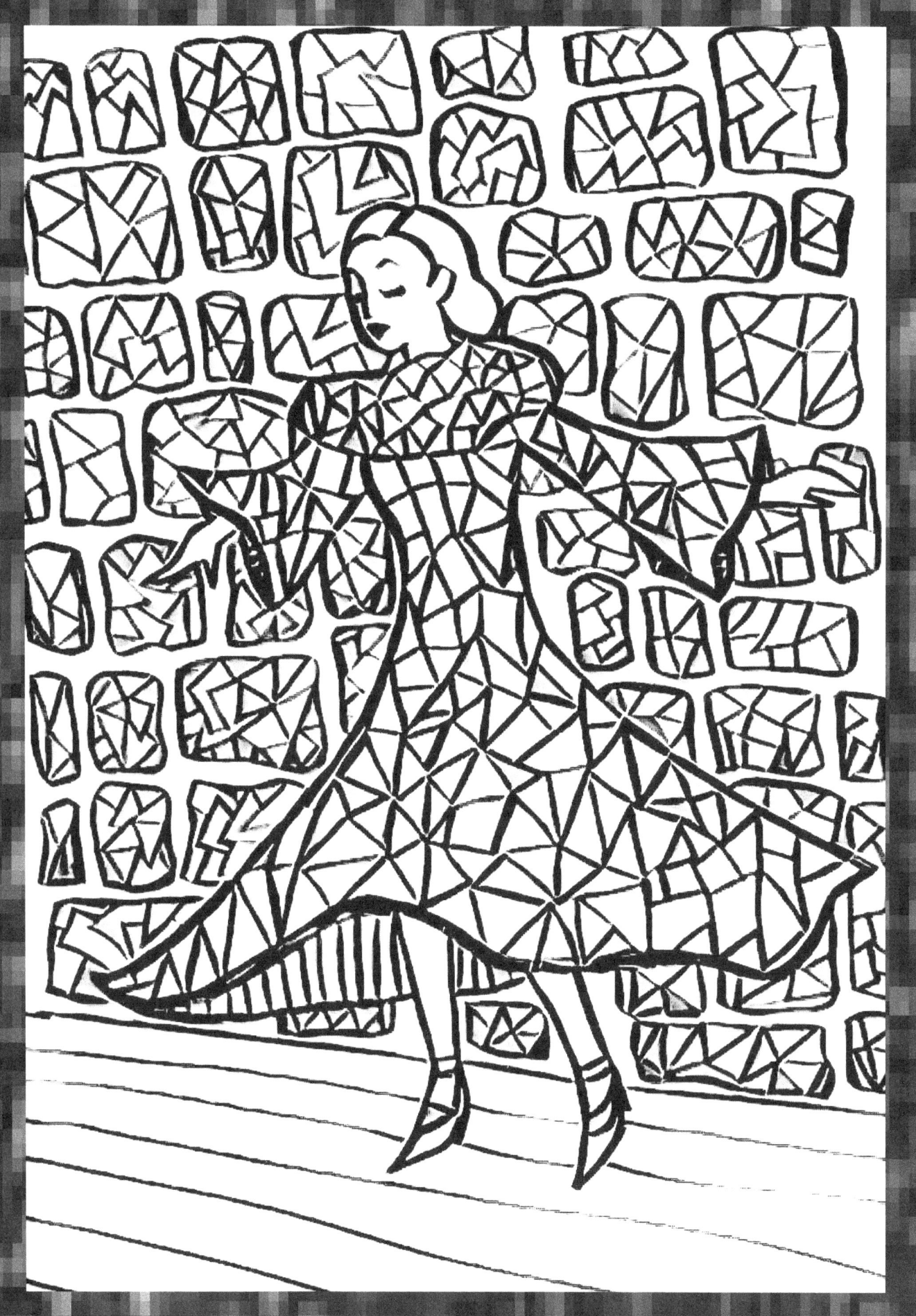

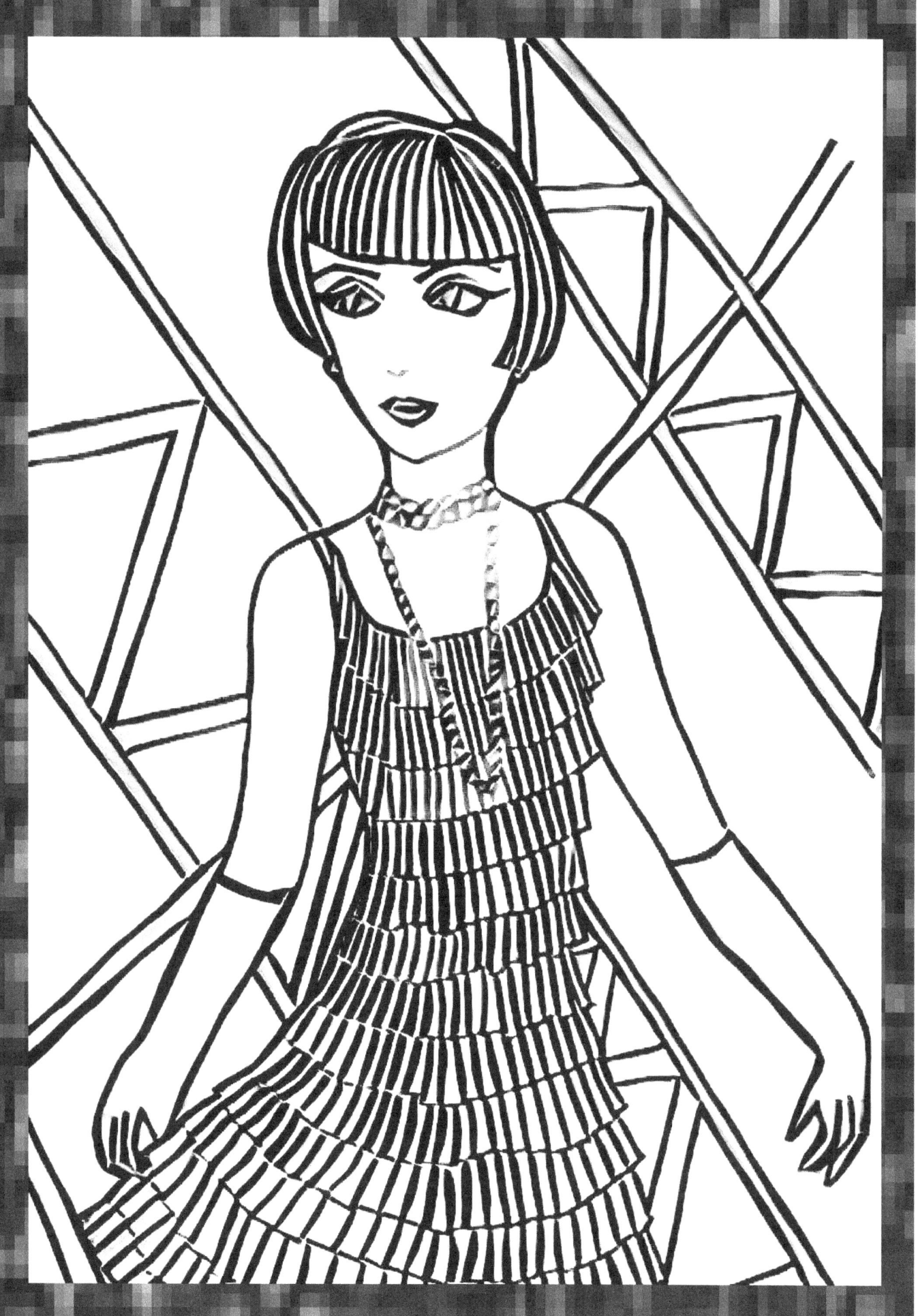

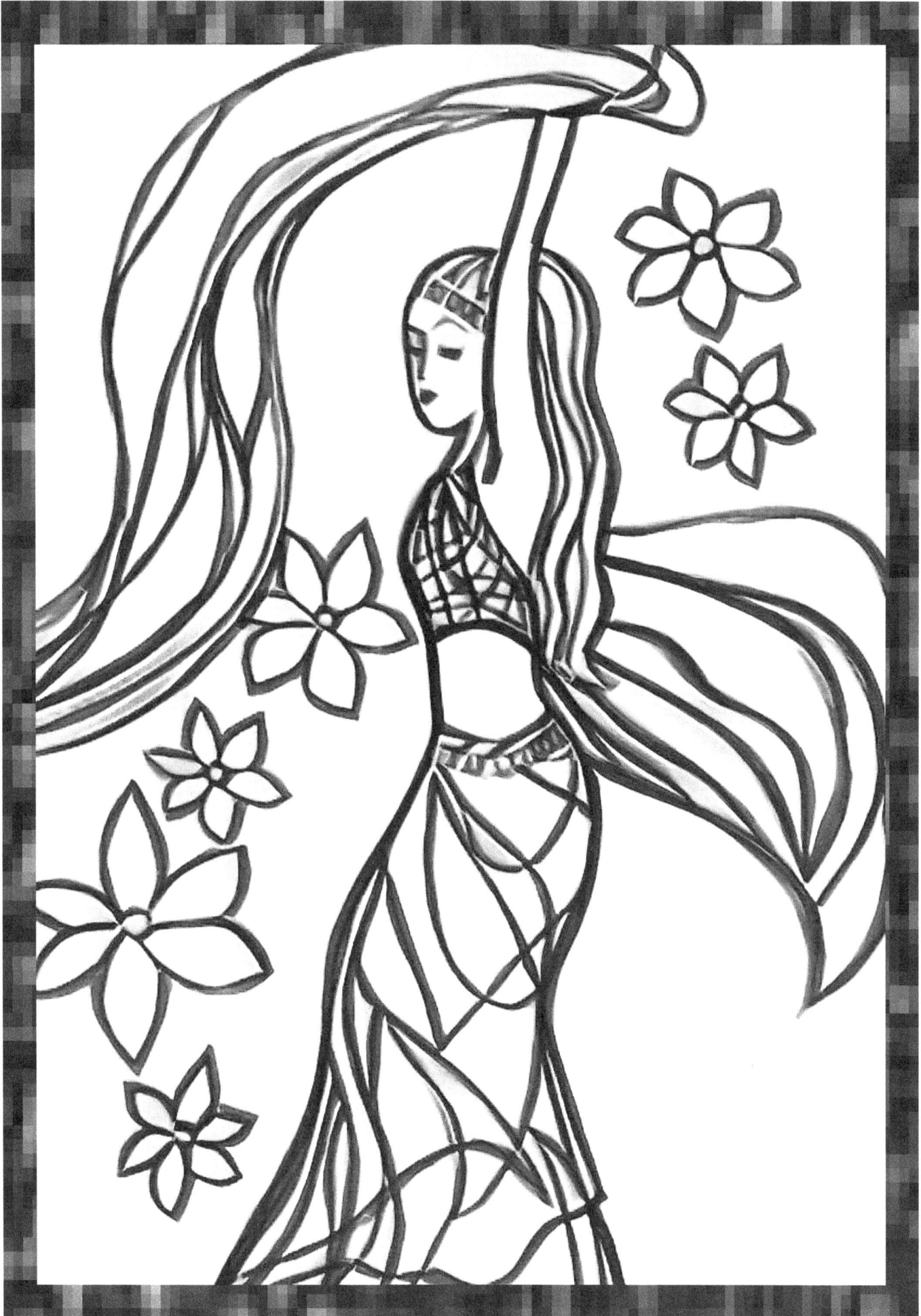

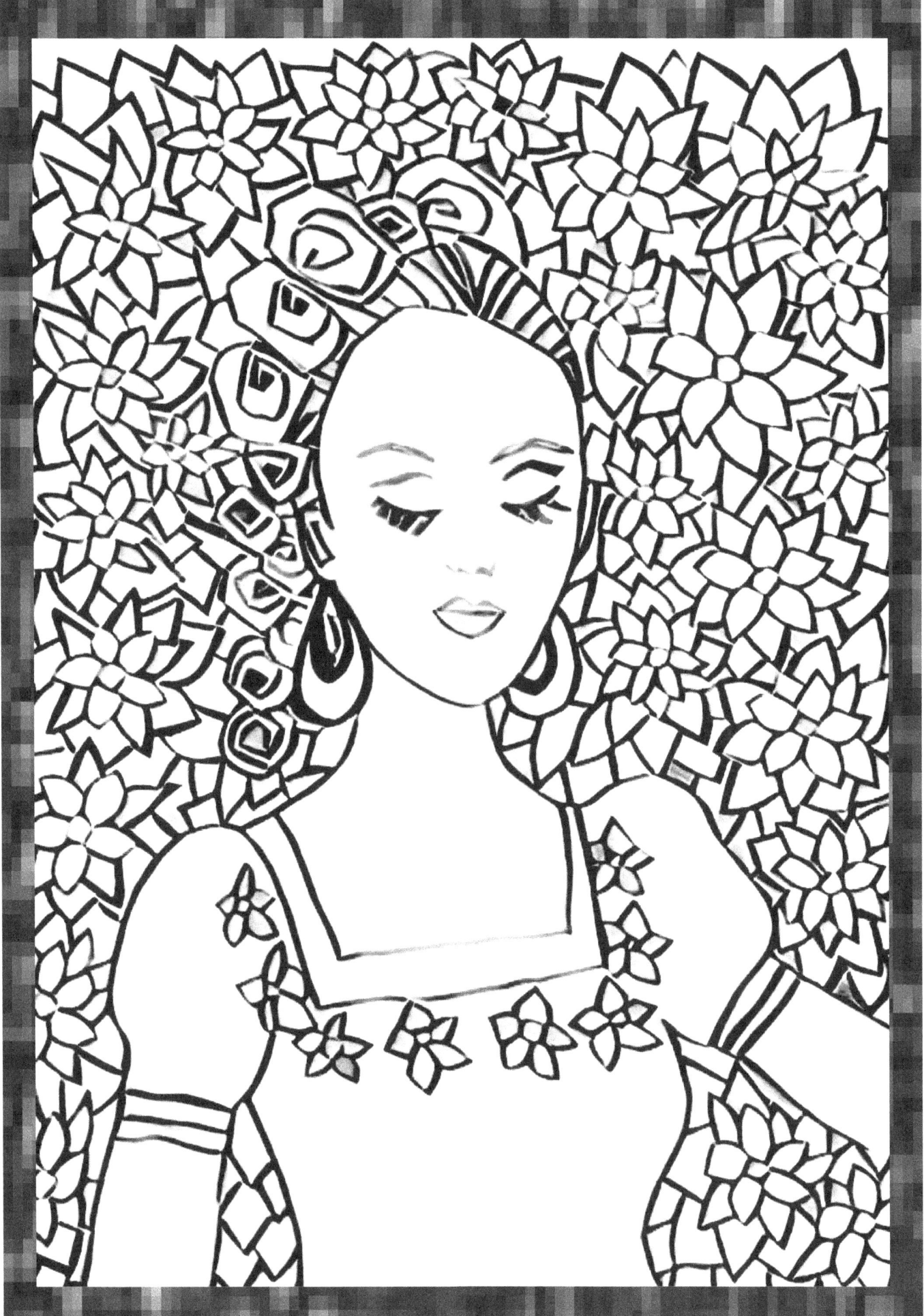

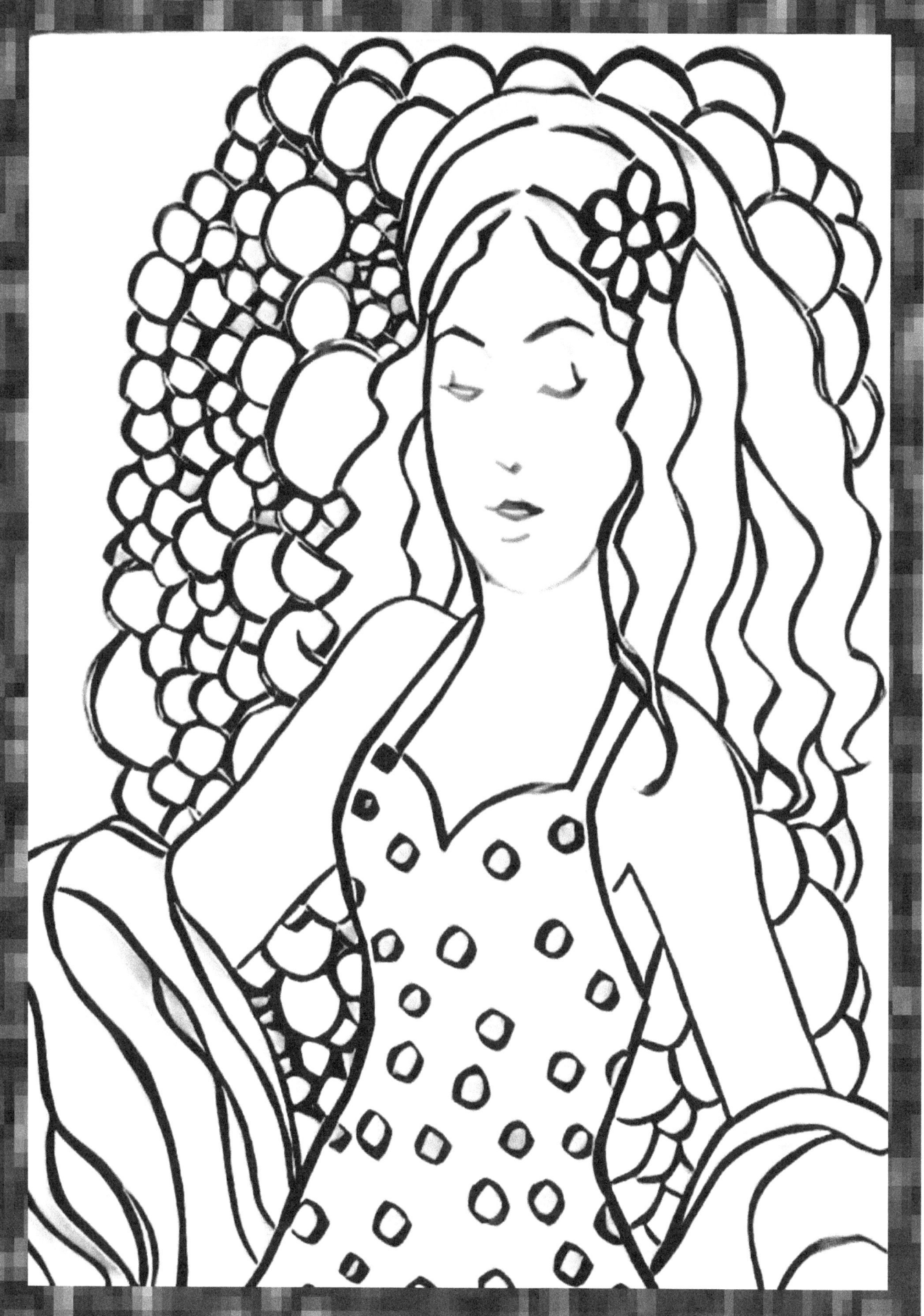

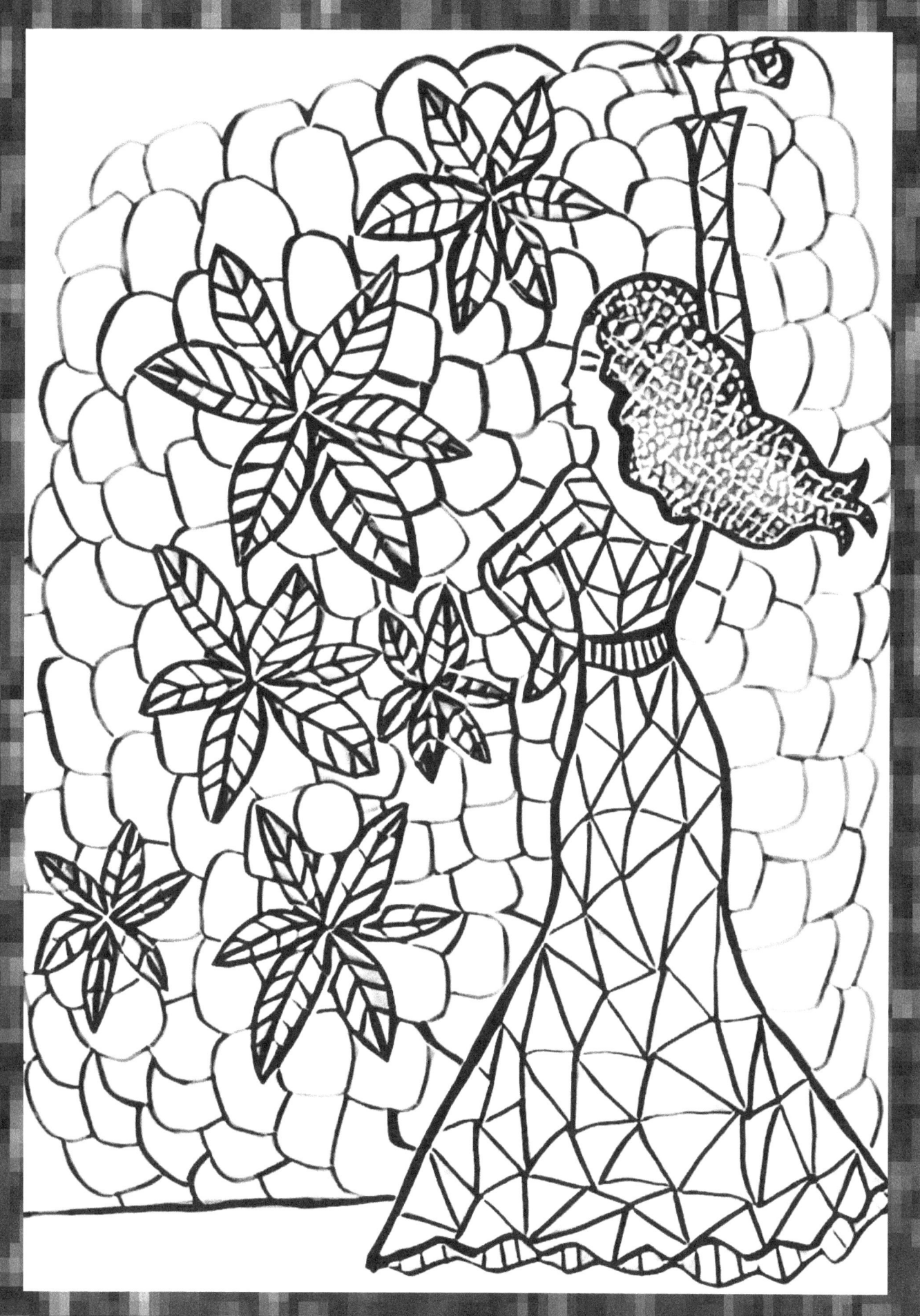

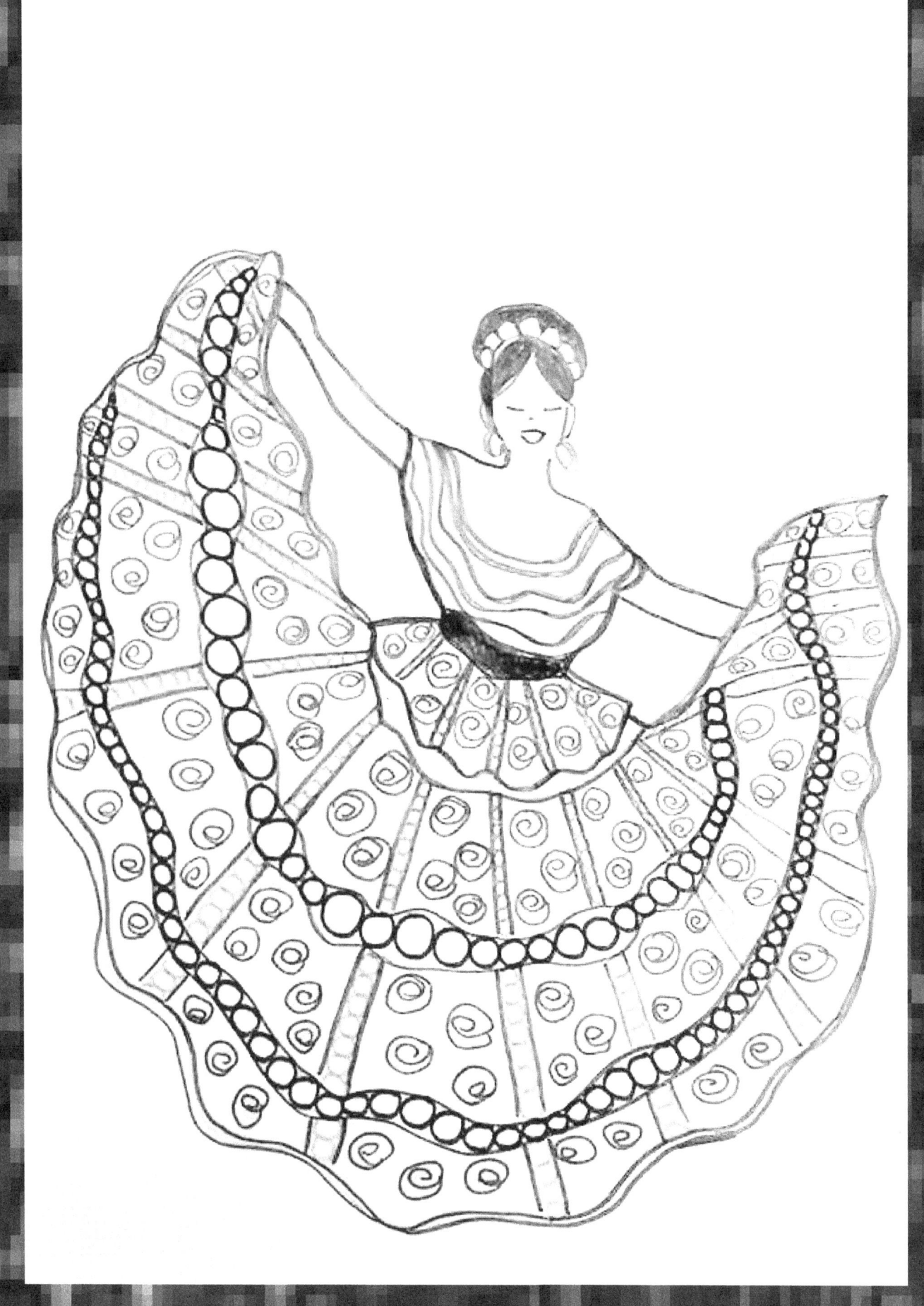

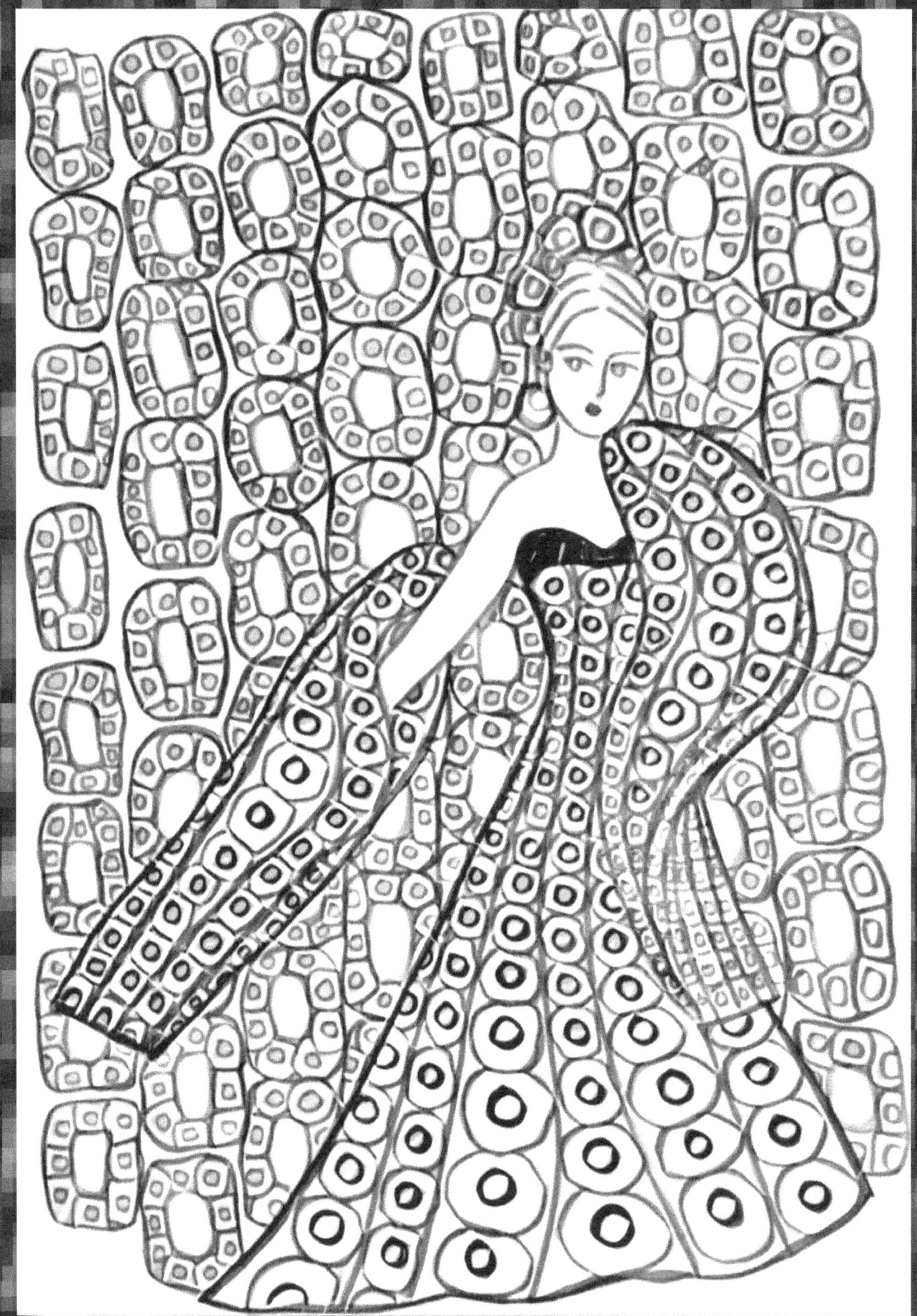

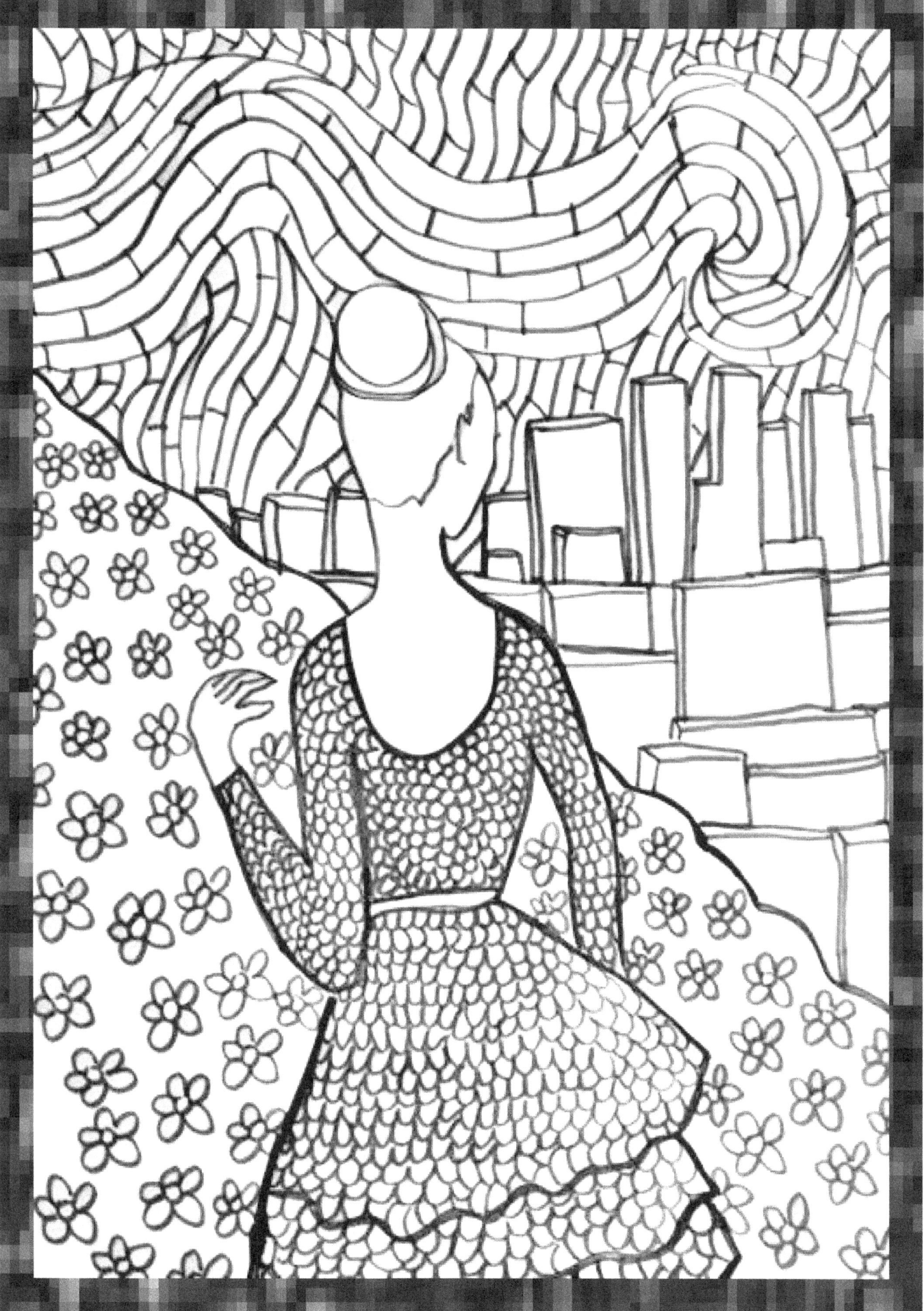

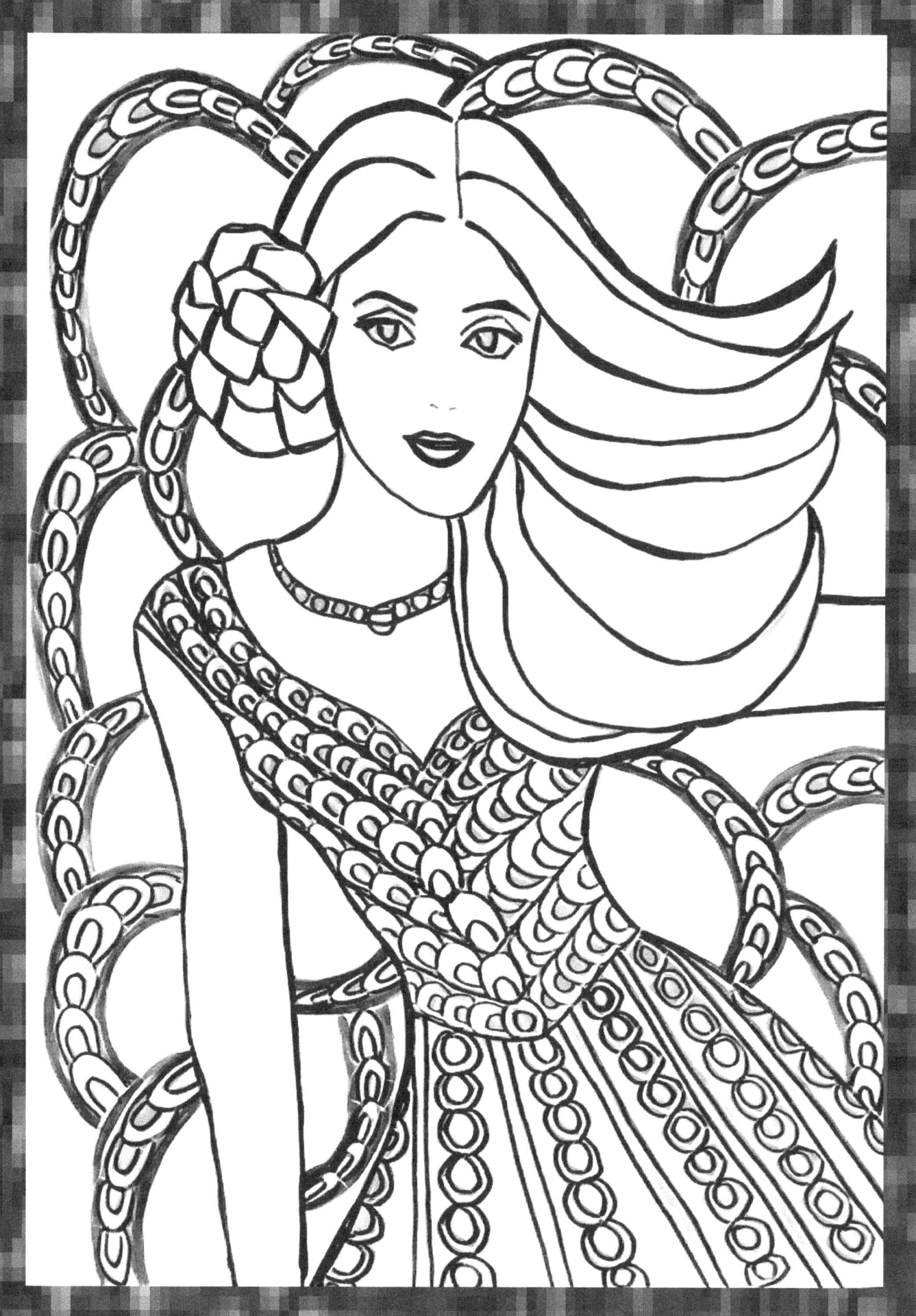

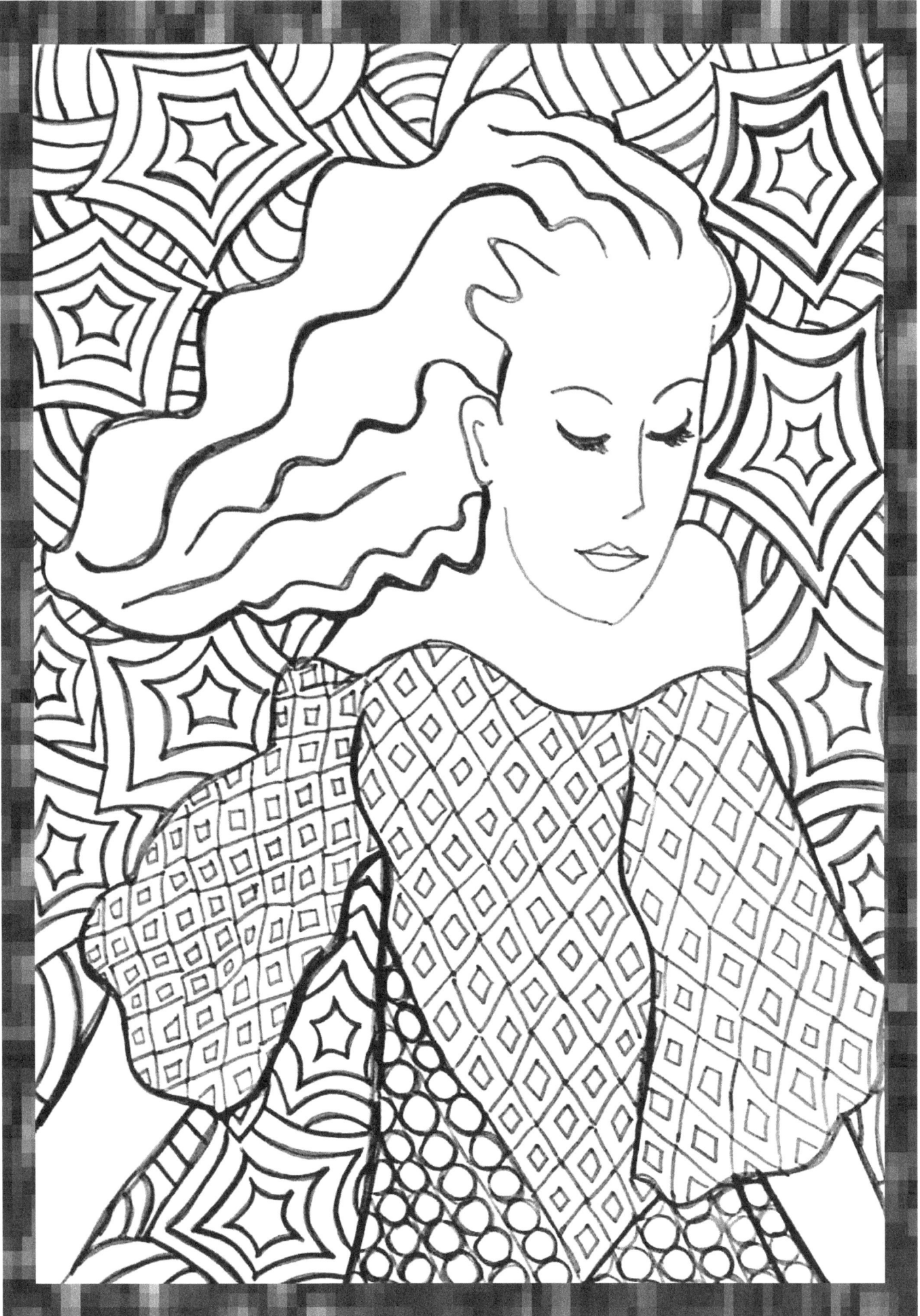

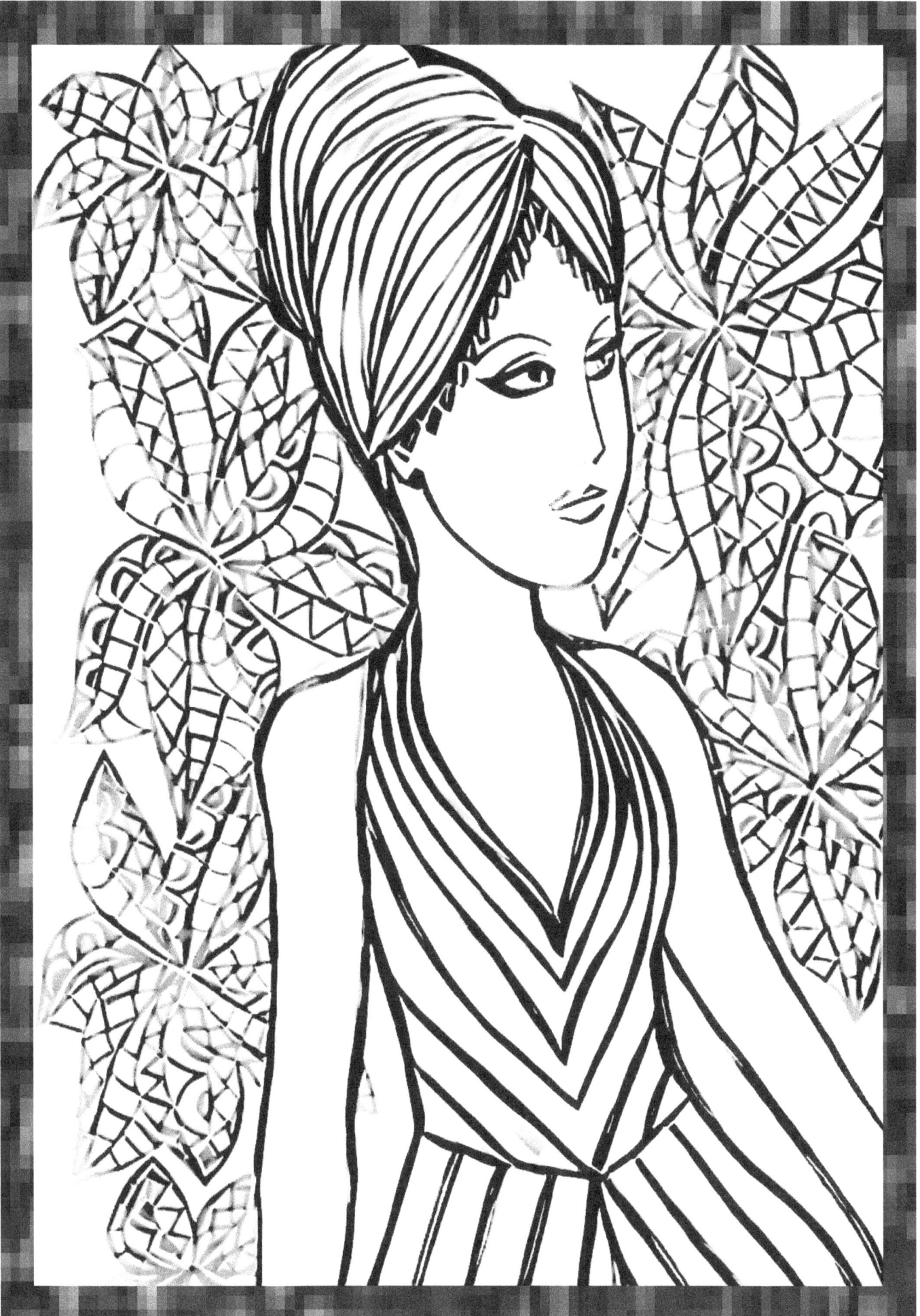

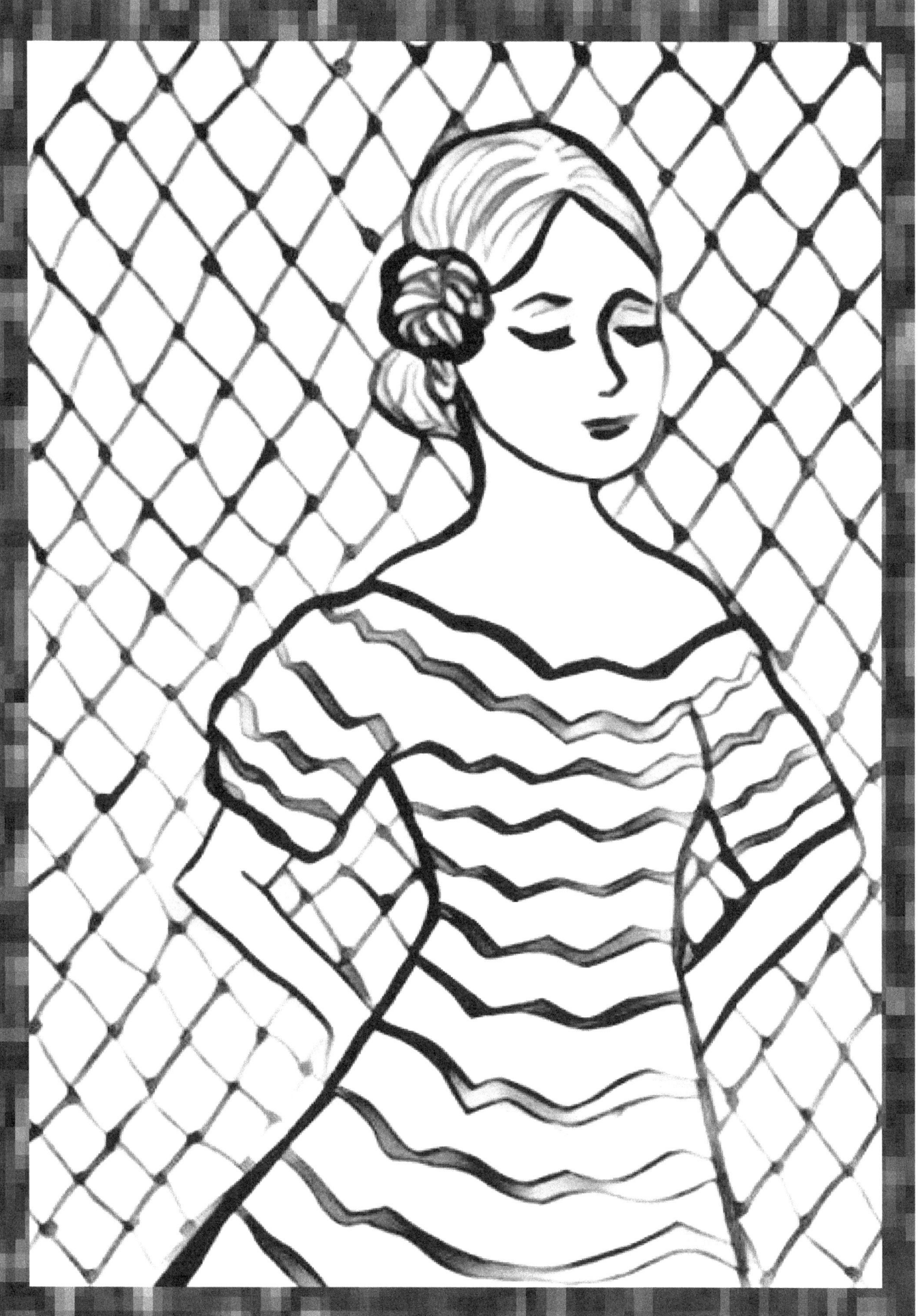

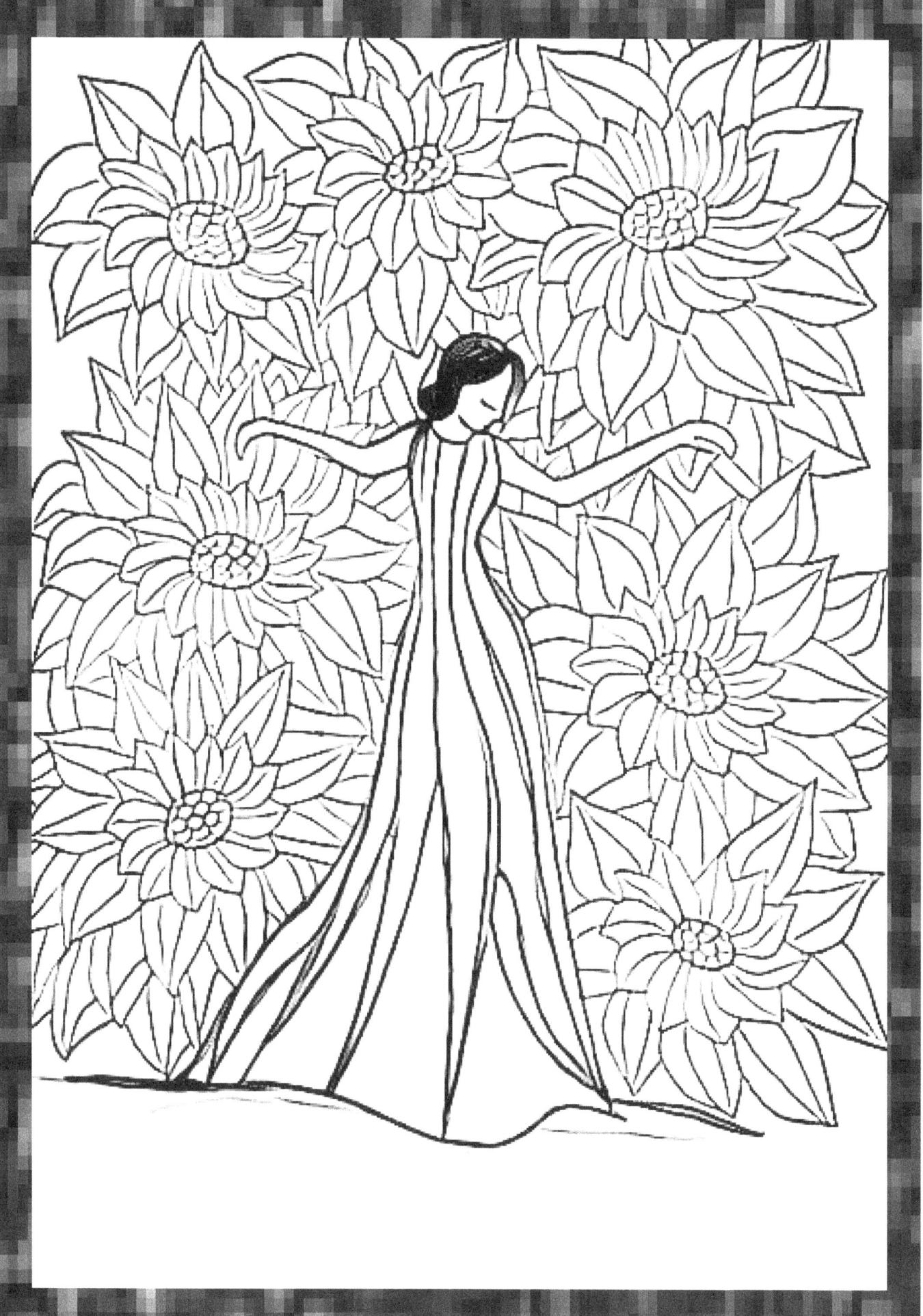

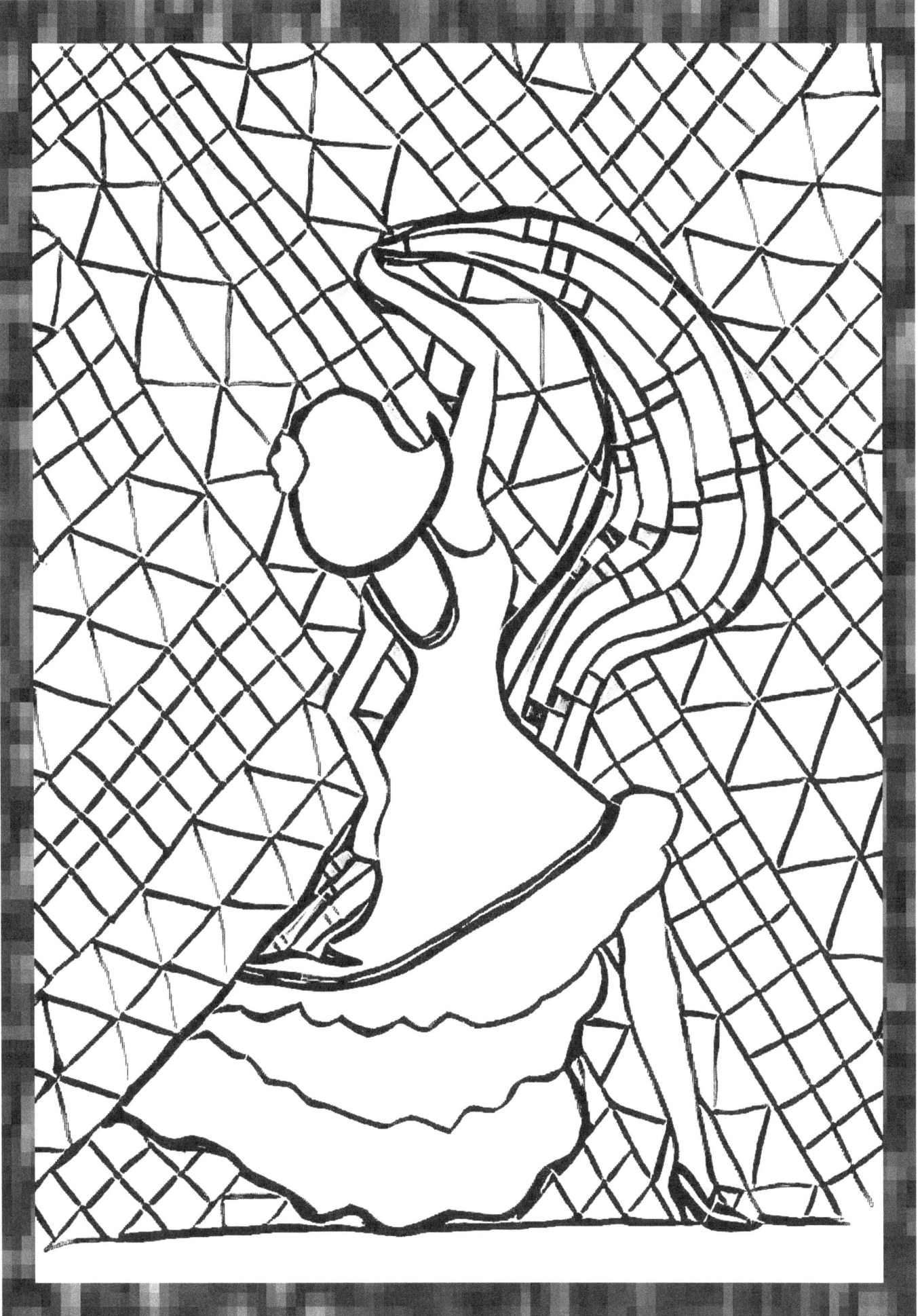

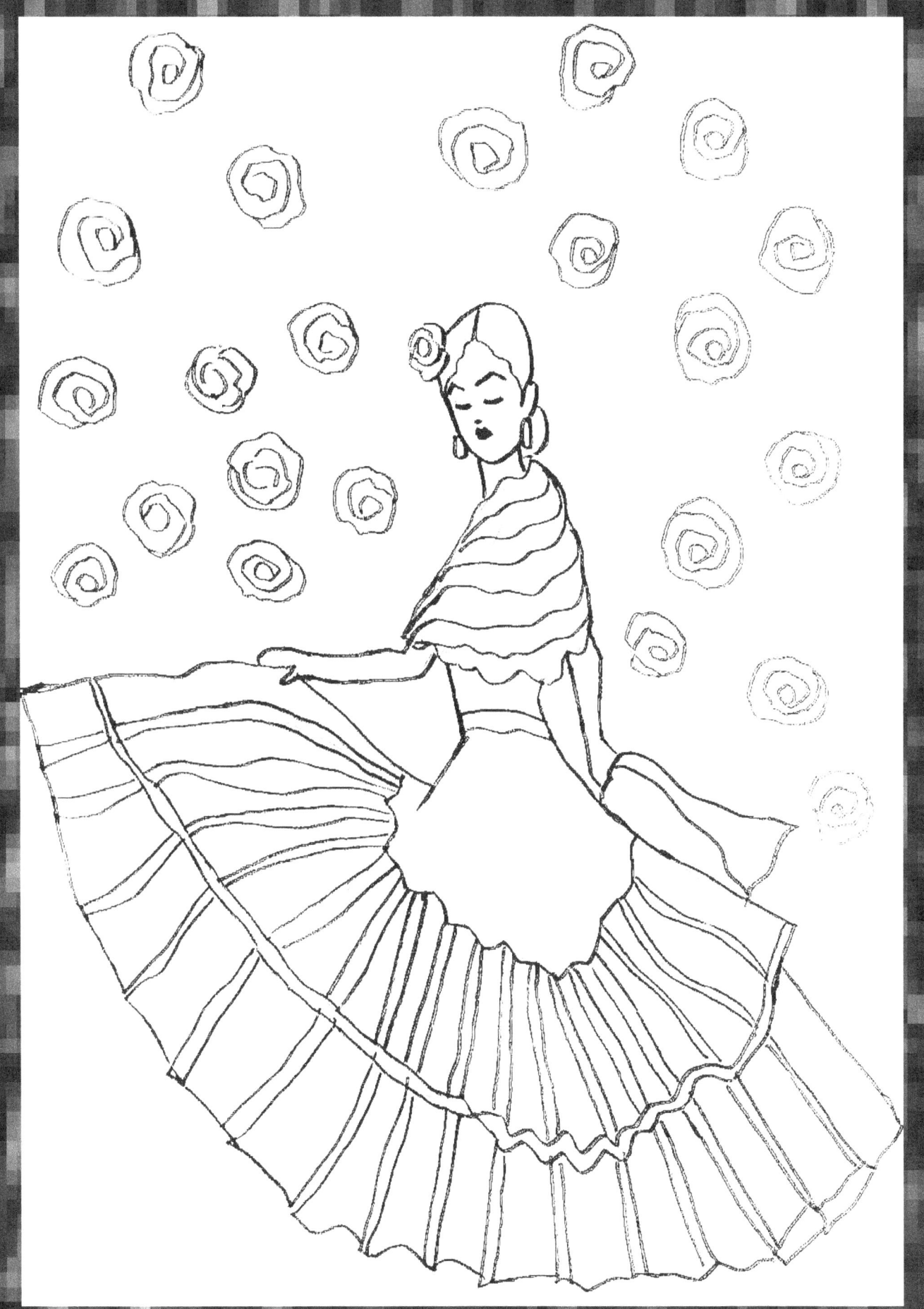

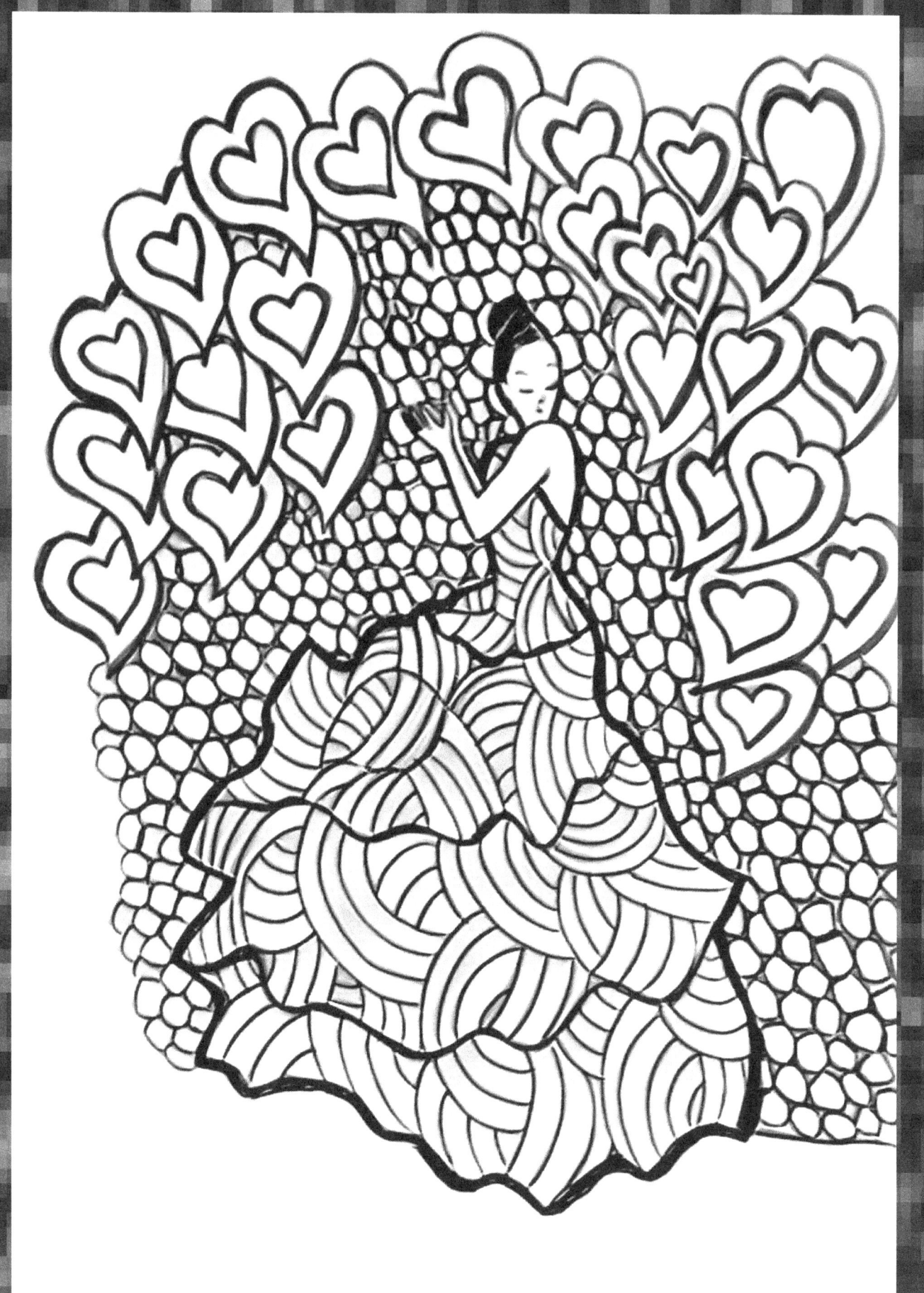